From one Heather
to another Heather –
Enjoy the journey –
Love, H



# The Quest of the Light Knights

Written and illustrated
by Heather I. Niderost

THE QUEST OF THE LIGHT KNIGHTS


Written and illustrated by Heather I. Niderost

ISBN 978-0-9809016-0-3

Book Design by Del Carry (mdtcommunications.com)

First Printing 2014



For permission requests, or where to get this book, email the publisher, at niderost@sympatico.ca

Library and Archives Canada Cataloguing in Publication

Niderost, Heather I. (Heather Isabel), 1940-, author
The quest of the light knights / Heather I. Niderost.

Includes index.
ISBN 978-0-9809016-0-3 (pbk.)

1. Religions--History--Juvenile literature. I. Title.

B92.N53 2014 j200 C2014-907145-0

Printed in the USA

*This book is dedicated*
*to my dear friend Navid Naimi*
*and to my grandchildren and their children.*

FROM THE BAHÁ'Í WRITINGS

*O contending peoples and kindreds of the earth!*
*Set your faces towards unity,*
*And let the radiance of its light shine upon you ...*
*There can be no doubt whatever that the peoples of the world,*
*Of whatever race or religion,*
*Derive their inspiration from one heavenly Source,*
*And are the subjects of one God.*
*The difference between the ordinances under which they abide*
*Should be attributed to the varying requirements*
*Of the age in which they were revealed ...*
*Cleave unto that which draweth you together and uniteth you.*

— *Bahá'u'lláh*

# TABLE OF CONTENTS


INTRODUCTION

1 SOPHIE ARRIVES . . . 11

2 THE LIGHT KNIGHTS . . . 16

3 WHAT'S A LIGHT-BODY? . . . 22

4 THE QUEST . . . 27

5 TIME-TRAVELLING . . . 30

6 SPIRIT IS THE FIRE . . . 35

7 THE MYSTERY OF THE PYRAMIDS . . . 39

8 THE LAND BETWEEN THE RIVERS . . . 43

9 THE GOD OF ABRAHAM . . . 47

10 THE COVENANT . . . 52

11 THE STORY OF JOSEPH . . . 55

12 ENTER MOSES . . . 58

13 EXODUS: THE ENDLESS SINAI JOURNEY . . . 62

14 ZOROASTER . . . 66

15 ENTER KRISHNA . . . 71

16 THE BUDDHA . . . 75

17 THE GREAT SILK ROAD . . . 80

18 JESUS APPEARS . . . 85

19 A MIRACLE . . . 91

20 MUHAMMAD THE PROPHET . . . 95

21 WHAT ABOUT THE AMERICAS? . . . 103

22 DEGANAWIDA . . . 107

23 QUETZACOATL . . . 112

24 THE BÁB . . . 118

25 BAHÁ'U'LLÁH, THE GLORY OF GOD . . . 124

26 AWAKENING THE WORLD . . . 130

27 THE GROUND RULES OF THE KINGDOM . . . 135

28 THE COVENANT COMES HOME . . . 142

29 THE COVENANT FLIES FREE . . . 147

30 THE KINGDOM UNFOLDS . . . 151

31 FAITH IS LIFE . . . 158

THOUGHTS AND THANKS . . . 161

END NOTES . . . 163

FURTHER READING . . . 164

ABOUT THE AUTHOR . . . 165

OTHER BOOKS BY AUTHOR . . . 167

# INTRODUCTION

## BIRTH OF A BOOK

We are on board *Spindrift*, our venerable old sailing sloop, skimming sedately along the Ottawa River, my husband Adrian at the helm, enjoying the countryside as it slips quietly by. My mind is busy; it is a-buzz with an idea, the germ of a book which constantly pesters me, that seeks to be born.

I am thinking about the dilemma of young people today who have had no formal religious training. Their parents have pulled up anchor, they see religion as old-hat, passé, the cause of more strife than good, something we can do without, and so they have set their faces to the winds of life, trusting their own judgment. But, I feel that inherited religion gave answers to big questions, gave values, gave a standard by which we could decide between right and wrong, at once a moral anchor and a reliable compass to navigate the world. If this spiritual compass is lacking in the psyche of the child, what happens? I feel that our youth are adrift, searching. The daunting winds of conflict, questions, and hard choices are blowing, the seas are whipping up. Does a reliable spiritual compass exist to traverse the perils of today?

So, here I am, teetering on the cusp of my 70's, and I look out at this same world and yearn to convey a lifetime of discovery. As a mother of five, a grandmother, and now a great-grand, I feel a wee bit feeble for the task! And yet there is this urgency welling up, bubbling to the surface of my mind. If I can offer a treasure to our youth, I simply must do it.

Perhaps it all began with my fascination with anthropology. I always loved that wonderful science that demonstrates beyond a doubt that religion has been central to human civilization since the beginning of time. It expresses the very heart of every culture. Through my mind swirls the vista of humanity evolving from its far distant, fascinating animistic infancy of spiritual integration with nature, up through the eons and on through its spiritual childhood of tribal traditions with their rules and regulations, on to powerful universal creeds that burst the bonds of geographic limitations, the harbingers of our turbulent spiritual adolescence of exercising willpower and choices, until now where we verge on the age of maturity, a time demanding very rational, cohesive, and world-embracing solutions. We find that all these levels of religious complexity, from tribal to global, co-exist today. It is a rich and beautiful banquet of culture, but inevitably very conflicted. How can we sort it all out, put our attitudes and values in order, and not suffer from massive indigestion? We are not only ready for an overarching creed to pull this planet together, we desperately need it.

This is *The Quest*, a mad and wonderful journey of three youth in search of spiritual answers to today's conflict and chaos. The journey reveals a silver thread, a 'Promise', that runs through our entire human history ultimately leading us to a solution that will rescue humanity from the jaws of total insanity. It is a huge gallop through time, but it is much more. The heroes of this epic—Lumina, Eric and Sophie—have arrived in the next world of existence, the 'Light World', as I have dubbed it, where, we are told, all the questions arising from our earthly lives will be answered. In my mental mulling, the idea took root of using the Light World as the setting for our story, because I felt it essential to show that our Earth World and the Light World are not separated, that there is a vital connection, one that we must recognize and address. Let me explain further.

## SETTING THE SCENE

Over 20 years ago I wrote a book for children, *The Light World*, following our son Eric's tragic accident and death at the age of 10, just before his 11th birthday. It was a book based on the Bahá'í teachings dealing with life after death, about the journey of the soul, a story of joy and adventure. I needed to share the many extraordinary experiences that surrounded our Eric's death, as well as all the knowledge forthcoming from the Bahá'í scriptures. Added to that, I had also miscarried a baby before Eric's conception. Some years ago, a very dear friend had a dream in which 'Lumina' appeared as Eric's brother, this miscarried baby, who had grown into boyhood in the Light World. How appropriate, I thought, that he should be called Lumina, as he had been born straight into that 'ocean of light', completely by-passing this earthly experience. The name has taken hold in my mind and become inseparable from him. It seems to evoke mystery and wonder. I firmly believe that, as the Bahá'í scriptures tell us, Lumina has been progressing, 'growing up' in that world of existence, and that he was there to help his brother Eric when he arrived so unexpectedly. Of course, that led me to imagine them off on all sorts of adventures together, conjured-up visions of a realm completely beyond our comprehension and yet so vividly alive and dancing in my mind.

Although this is definitely a work of fiction, the narrative has been inspired by the wonderful teachings of Bahá'u'lláh, the founder of the Bahá'í Faith. We are told that the soul arrives in the next world of existence in the state of purity it achieved in the Earth World. This gives us pause, because we all arrive in different spiritual states, some happy and luminous, and some far from happy and luminous. We are told that when we arrive in the Light World we still have to untangle our problems from our earthly lives, face what our hands have done, and resolve these barriers to our progress. Once free of this baggage, we are told that the soul is able to go on, to continue growing spiritually, until it attains the presence of God. Now, Bahá'u'lláh's concept of God is the universal God of all religions.[1] So I, in my mulling, decided that GOD (in capital letters) somehow evokes this universal principle.

To go on, it only makes sense to me that we have a great deal to learn when we first arrive in the Light World, especially if we have had no particular spiritual preparation beforehand. This inspired the character of feisty Sophie. Her questions abound, and being a very enterprising lassie, she's game! She joins forces with Lumina and Eric, who have dubbed themselves 'Light Knights', and she proceeds to develop her spiritual 'wings', sweeping us along with her. Like so many youth today, Sophie is searching for answers to the overwhelming problems facing us in the Earth World, as well as a way to reach out and help.

So, without further ado, let's join *The Quest.* Let's see what Sophie and the Light Knights unravel and reveal.

# 1 SOPHIE ARRIVES

Welcome to the Light World! Imagine you are leaping into the next world of existence, into an ocean of light. Shut your eyes and stretch your minds. Try to visualize this world of glorious light, invisible beyond our earthly eyes, of shifting, shimmering shafts of colour, dancing, spreading, contracting, gliding … an ethereal world throbbing with a musical cadence that sings and wafts in the limitless atmosphere, like a symphony of the heavens. Imagine 'light-bodies', myriads of shapes, flashing, blinking in and out, some bright, some dimmer, some dull, and that they communicate their thoughts.

"Leaping lizards!" shouts Lumina. "Here comes our new recruit for the Light Knights! Duck, Eric!"

PPHHhhhSSsssssstttTT

A wild-eyed, agitated, rosy light-body swooshes to a skithering halt in front of the two boys, corkscrew ringlets of light bobbing madly on her head.

"Whoa-ho, there, young lady … and welcome to the Light World!" says Lumina, as they recover from her topsy-turvy arrival.

"Whew!" she says breathlessly. "Hi, I'm Sophie! Are you Lumina and Eric?

I'm supposed to report to Lumina and Eric." She eyes them expectantly.

"I thought Lumina would be a girl, but you're both boys!" They grin and manage a nod, watching Sophie's rosy light pulse. She's having one heck of a time settling down.

"Oh, good-good-good! I'm so relieved I found you," she swivels around, fascinated by the kaleidoscopic flow of colours, the light sheeting and flashing about her. "It's all so new and strange here. And just look at this light-body of mine ... whoooeee!"

She spins about, sending out rosy sparks, giggling at it all. "And I just love these crazy ringlets." They bob some more. She sweeps out her light-arms, swooshing more sparks. "Look at all this! It's so crazy busy here, and people say it's eternal rest? They haven't a clue!"

Her bright brown light-eyes are popping as she bubbles on, so Lumina and Eric just back off and let her work off her head of steam. Boy!

"I just can't believe I'm here, really here, and talking to you .... Well, aaaah ... sort of transmitting?"

Sophie shakes her light-head as she gathers her wits, and finally she turns quietly to face them. "You see, guys, I died of leukemia. There I was lying in bed for months and months, thinking, and going bald, just so boring, and I kept having these flashes of another world, one full of light—just like this!

"Well, when I tried to explain it, nobody understood. They figured I was dreaming, or it was those horrible drugs I was on. I had soooo many questions about what would happen to me when I died, and nobody, I mean *nobody*, could answer them. They'd just roll their eyes and look up at the ceiling; or worse, they'd start crying. Or they'd say, 'There, there, dear' and pat my hand. So frustrating!" Sophie shakes her light-head dolefully as she remembers it all.

She raises her light-eyes, round with sudden, desperate yearning.

"I've been zeroing in on my family ever since I arrived here, trying to let them know I'm totally fine. I just have to get through to them; they're having such a tough time. And I don't want them to cry—I can't *stand* seeing them cry. Oh, guys! I really miss my Mom and Dad!"

Like a flickering light bulb, poor Sophie's rosy light wavers and throbs, expressing her anguish. Lumina and Eric close in and gently comfort her with their light-arms. They understand.

Now Lumina finally has a chance to take charge. He's a taller, brilliant-yellow light-body with a stunning 'afro' of light shimmering around his head; his light-eyes flash a glorious sea-green. Gliding back he spreads his light-arms wide and says, "Sophie, we're here for you, we're here. I'm Lumina, and this handsome young spark is Eric."

Eric, who's nearly Lumina's height, but not quite so brilliant, bows gallantly, his thatch of light-locks cascading over twinkly sky-blue light-eyes, and a welcoming grin splits his light-face as Lumina continues.

"I know it's not easy at first, Sophie, but you'll adjust and get used to it all; and you won't ever lose contact with your earth family—that's a promise."

Lumina's quiet words do the trick, and Sophie visibly starts to settle down.

Eric pipes up. "It's my turn, Sophie. I arrived here a few earth-years ago, about the same age as you—eleven, right?" Her light-ringlets bob. "That was after a biking accident, and you talk about a shock! No warning at all. Just bang! Zoom down the light tunnel I went, and poof—here I was. I mean, I had no time to think. And nobody could prepare me either. So I just arrived. And Lumina here looked after me. This Light World's one fantastic place, eh? Everything here is light. Man, just look at those fabulous colours!"

Eric is blinking in different shades of yellow as he speaks. "And music! Sophie, do you hear the music? It just blows and sings around."

Sophie nods, lifting her light-face, tingling all over.

"We communicate, too; our minds work, don't they?"

"That's for darn sure!" Sophie nods emphatically at Eric, her brown light-eyes dancing with excitement.

"And, Sophie," adds Lumina, "believe it or not, Eric's my earth-brother."

Her light-eyes widen. "That's so cool!" She eyes the two brothers. They really don't look at all alike.

"So, I have a story, too. Our mum miscarried me before Eric was born, so I skipped the Earth World completely and landed here really, really young. But I didn't stay that way, did I? Look at me now!" He straightens up quite majestically. His gorgeous, golden light-body is something to behold, all right. Sophie is fascinated.

"So, I was adopted and named Lumina, meaning 'light'. Neat, I think, and I grew up here. My light-family took me under their wing, taught me everything I know. Then, after his bike accident, Eric arrived, and he joined up with me.

"You see, Sophie, I have always kept in touch. There's an amazing bond that connects us to our Earth World families, a sort of 'crazy-glue' of love that never disappears. Do you follow me? My Earth World family will meet me for the very first time here in the Light World, and then we'll be together for all time."

He pauses to see the effect of all this on her.

Sophie is awed by his revelation. A miscarriage? Babies go on ... and keep growing up .... "Oh, Lumina, what a story."

She reaches out to them with her light-hands, and the three of them have a quiet moment of just being together, fusing their energy. "Whew. I feel such a weight lifting off me. I feel so alive. That's it! I feel *alive*!"

Sophie lifts up her light-face. She then wraps her light-arms around herself and looks about, watching the light show, gazing in wonder at the singing undulations of colour, drinking in this extraordinary new world she has entered.

# 2 THE LIGHT KNIGHTS

Sophie is just realizing that the gloriously beautiful, shifting shafts of light remind her of the northern lights in the Earth World, when her attention is drawn to strangely dim light-bodies eddying in and out.

"Why are light-bodies all different brightnesses?" She points. "Look—some are really dim, sort of sad."

"That's a really good question." Lumina settles in to explain. "You see, we all arrive in the Light World with different baggage from our earth lives. We're all bundles of experiences, some happy and some not happy at all, and we have to face all the things we've done with our earth lives when we get here. That's when we realize that our attitudes control our light, that if we're kind and considerate our volts go up, and if we're selfish and mean our volts go down … as though our light-bodies are on 'dimmer' switches. Life is full of choices, every step of the way, and we have to take responsibility for our choices, for our own light."

Lumina pauses to make sure Sophie's following him. "So, those light-bodies that are kind of dim, well, they have some sad baggage. They can remember everything now, and they're working it out so their light will grow stronger."

Sophie nods her light-head slowly, gazing about in sympathy. "I guess

I'm lucky to be this gorgeous pink, huh? I had lots of time to talk about things and sort things out before I came."

Eric turns to his brother, very serious. "Suicide really bothers me, Lumina. I feel a deep, deep pain .... I feel so awfully sorry for people who commit suicide, especially kids. They must see suicide as an escape, that they can just fly away and forget everything. But they can't, can they? Their problems keep dogging them till they get solved. It's only when we arrive in this Light World that we really grasp what an amazing gift our earth life was, our own unique human life. It's *here* that we understand its value more clearly, much more clearly, than we ever could in the Earth World."

"Yes," continues Lumina. "Eric, it's here that we realize the important opportunities we missed, especially if we shortened our time on Earth. Believe me, that's a hard, hard thing for those souls to face when they arrive here. And, that's one *big* reason why prayers are so important." Lumina is very serious. "Prayers are a pure, spiritual force, channels of power working in the Earth World, in the Light World, and between the worlds."

Lumina sweeps his light-arms around. "So, prayers from the Earth World reach us here in the Light World. They have a transforming power, like an electric current that switches us from negative to positive. They give us healing, deep-down healing."

"And how!" exclaims Eric. "When I arrived here I was totally unprepared, and then my whole life flashed by, like a movie clicking away, eh, Sophie?"

Sophie nods. She knows exactly what he means.

"I had to take in everything I'd done in my earth life," Eric continues. "And I wasn't too pleased with myself, believe me. I mean, I was just a kid and it never occurred to me that everything I did mattered so much. I desperately wanted to clear the slate. Then those prayers just welled up from the Earth World, surrounding me with love and forgiveness, transforming me."

Sophie's hanging on Eric's every word. So this is how it works ....

"I wasn't this golden boy when I arrived, y'know. I had some tidying up to do." Eric's remembering it all. Then he smiles at her. "You've felt the prayers too, eh, Sophie?"

"Oooooh, you bet I've felt them! They come like showers of light and just wash over me. They feel like 'love showers'!" She's gleeful at the realization.

Lumina beams at the two of them. "So, here we go, team! We three are the 'Light Knights'!"

"Whaaat? Night-lights?" Sophie's big, brown light-eyes dance with mischief.

That does it! Eric and Lumina dissolve into helpless laughter, their golden light-bodies belly and chime. Lord, she's fun!

"No, no, Sophie!" gasps Eric, hiccupping sparks. "We're *Light Knights*, like soldiers off on a special mission. You know—they used to wear shining armour and perform valiant deeds, all very noble." He throws out his light-chest in mock pride, and sweeps her a courtly bow. More sparks fly.

"Oh, *those* knights!" She's really enjoying herself.

"So, Sophie, when I arrived here and met up with my brother Lumina, I got my act together, charged up my positive volts, and we came up with the idea of the Light Knights, because we light-bodies have a mission. We can actually help people back in the Earth World. We're not really separated from that world at all, and that's how we zeroed in on *you*, Sophie."

Sophie's big brown light-eyes widen with amazement. "*Me*?"

"Yes, you! Lumina and I intercepted your questions, and that's why you had flashes of this world. And why you weren't afraid of dying."

"Oh my gosh! It was *you*? Oh, that's so ... so ... so absolutely *awesome*, you guys!" In her glee, she flings her light-arms around them, spinning the three of them into a whirl of light. It's all starting to make sense, real sense.

"So, are you game, Sophie?" Lumina asks, as he and Eric extricate themselves. "Are you game to be a Light Knight and join forces with Eric and me?"

Her rosy light pulses happily. Oh, sure, she's game! Out goes her light-hand, and the three of them fuse light-fingers in a solemn pact.

Lumina then spreads out his light-arms, in a gesture embracing the whole Light World. "So, Sophie, this is all yours now. We, the Light Knights, are going in search of the answers to all those questions you have buzzing around in your light-head, and then we, the intrepid Light Knights, will carry on and help the Earth World!"

"Questions!" bursts out Sophie, "Oh, boy! I have soooo many questions. I mean, the Earth World's in such a mess, and I just can't see how it'll *ever* get better. I used to think that grownups knew the answers, could solve anything. Then, lying in that hospital bed, I realized that if they had any clue at all, those huge problems wouldn't have existed in the first place! What a let-down *that* was! So depressing."

She sighs gustily. "So what's the point of it all? You've got mega-greedy people grabbing all the wealth, and the little guy just gets poorer and hungrier … and the forests are being cut down and disappearing … and all that belching, dirty smoke from billions of factories and trucks … and poisonous sprays wrecking the ozone layer … and then gucky garbage polluting our rivers and oceans and soil …."

Sophie's light pulses redder and redder as she rattles on angrily. She wants answers. "Do we just mess up the earth and leave? There's gotta be a better way, and I want to find it! Can *we* make a difference?" Her light-fists are planted on her light-hips.

Eric nods emphatically. "You bet, Sophie. But the real question for me is, can humanity as a whole wake up and make a lasting change in the way we behave? Can we stop being selfish and uncaring? I mean, everything, absolutely *everything*, needs to change. Our butting in and helping here and there isn't going to do much in the long run, eh? So, what's the key to changing the mind-set of humanity?"

"Eric's question is the big one, Sophie," says Lumina. "And we're going to find the answer. That's what I want to share with both of you, all the amazing things I've learned since I arrived here. I'm going to take us on a leap into the distant past, starting from the very beginning of the human journey, and then we'll follow the 'yellow brick road' to the 'Emerald City of Oz'."

Sophie gives him a quizzical look. We're off to Oz?

"Well, not really," Lumina laughs, "but it's kind of like that! I want to show you how we humans evolved over the eons and arrived at the stage we're at today in the Earth World. I think it's really important for us Light Knights to see the whole picture, to find out what all humans have in common. There's a great story to tell, Sophie, a mystery to unfold. And despite the dire situation today, there *is* light at the end of the tunnel, a wonderful future ahead for the Earth World—that I promise."

Sophie's suddenly all shivery, her sparkles seem to tinkle and chime. "I feel so tingly, like my light-body has goose-bumps! I feel like something big is going to happen, so powerful, so awesome … I feel like I'm on the edge of the Universe …."

"It's all yours, Sophie!" Eric grins.

# 3 WHAT'S A LIGHT-BODY?

Sophie suddenly sweeps her light-hands up and down through her column of light, her light-eyes dancing.

"Okay, so the first thing you'd better explain is this light-body of mine. I mean, how can I even think without a brain? And I do remember all my earth-life now. What an initiation that was, just like watching a movie—like you said, Eric! Lots of things I'd forgotten came back to me. I was even shown the effects of stuff I'd said or done; what an eye-opener *that* was! Those effects just ripple on and on forever, touching so many people."

Sophie waves into the distance, throwing off rosy sparks. "But, Eric, what am I now? *What am I*?" Sophie's light-eyes are big as saucers.

"Your gorgeous light-body's your soul, Sophie. Humans aren't just a fusion of an egg and sperm, y'know. There's an incredible life-force involved. Think of your soul as that life-force that causes the real 'atomic fusion'. Voila! A new person's created."

"Are you trying to tell me that this light-body was *always* the real me?"

"Exactly!" Eric grins. "Your light-body had an *in*-body experience in the Earth World and now it is *out*."

"And how!" Sophie pirouettes about, delighting in her light-bodiness.

"Okay, you two. Listen up!" says Lumina. "The light-body doesn't simply give life to the body cells, does it? No way! The light-body leaves the physical body, has a mind of its own that keeps on working, and here we are in the Light World. This marvellous light-body is what makes us truly human and not just highly intelligent animals."

"Weeell, that's what lots of people think we are—just really intelligent animals.… And sometimes nooot so intelligent either!" sputters Sophie.

"Yeah," says Eric, "and they sure don't believe this Light World exists, do they? They just brush it off, call it wishful thinking, 'pie-in-the-sky', a big sham." He sighs gustily, shaking his light-head.

"Well, it's pretty hard to explain, you know. Behind it all there is a *huge* Mystery," continues Lumina. "The way it was explained to me, there's a 'First Force', a 'Great Spirit', that's at work outside the physical universe. This Spirit has brought all the physical cosmos into being, and out of that evolved what we call life on Planet Earth: the minerals, plants, animals, and us. Everything's infused with a life-force, a 'spirit'. But, the human spirit or soul, the light-body, thinks and creates, independent of the laws of nature, transforming the world around it. It's amazing, and beyond our comprehension, beyond science. The light-body is just marvellous!"

Lumina's getting a bit carried away, trying to get the big picture into words. "The soul, the light-body, Sophie, is a reflection of that Great Spirit that created it."

He stops for a moment, allowing her some time for this idea to sink in.

"Ahaaaa," says Sophie, nodding slowly, "so that Great Spirit is what we call GOD." She suddenly straightens up. "Does that mean we are all connected to GOD somehow? And … and am I just some sort of weird puppet?"

Eric grins. "I don't think you're any weird puppet! You're speaking your own thoughts, so your light-body is you, the real you, the thinking you. But we do have that GOD-spark, so you've got to accept it, Sophie—you're simply *divine*!" He grins wickedly.

"Ooooh, tell him to stop, Lumina!" Sophie's just a wee bit rosier ....

"Okay, okay, you two, back to basics here. Imagine that GOD is the All-Knowing, Conscious Force that brought the universe into being—"

"Whoa, *conscious*?" Sophie jumps in. "Lumina, do you mean since *we* are conscious ... like awake ... aware ... then GOD is '*Awareness-plus*'? Like ... *GOD* existed before everything else? Thought it all up?" Sophie's thoughts zing away, she's unable to put it all into words. Who could?

"Exactly, Sophie! You're getting it! Right from the get-go GOD wanted some part of this cosmos to know Him, to tie in with Him and love Him back. So He created the human soul with the power to think. And this power of thought is full of curiosity. We wonder about GOD, the Source of our being. So, we *consciously* try to connect up with Him. And, when we do that, our souls awaken to a whole new world of possibilities. Our souls are turned on, our light goes up. Out of our curiosity come questions about the meaning of life. A new journey of discovery begins."

"Oh, my!" mouths Sophie

"And Sophie, that's it! Here you are asking questions. It's a part of your soul, your light-body. And you're wide awake at the switch!"

Lumina is rather proud of himself. This is real work!

"Let me get this straight, Lumina. You're telling me that my body was sort of like a vehicle, a car or something, in the Earth World and I, Sophie-light-body, was the driver?"

Eric jumps in. "Yeah, and try this idea, Sophie: The brain of the earth-body is like an amazing computer taking in the world around it through the senses—the eyes, ears, nose, taste and touch—feeding information to the light-body, which is like the intelligent operator at work. And the mind is the connection, a kind of morphing program going on when you get the two working together. Something like that. The conscious mind is part of the light-body, and survives the earth-body's death. Does that make sense?"

Sophie is thinking hard. "Soooo ... so my earth-body was like a cage and my soul like a bird stuck inside .... Oh wow!" Her light-eyes pop. "A bird has wings, wants to fly free, up and out, sing in the sunshine, feel the Spirit lifting its wings. And it really can't do these things till it gets out of that cage!" She's flapping her light-arms in complete abandon; sparks scatter.

"Beautiful, Sophie! Lumina, she's got it!" Eric bounces with delight, throwing off a few sparks of his own. Lumina just shakes his light-head. What a bunch!

"Whoa! Simmer down, you two. Sophie, your 'bird-spirit' *did* start to fly in the Earth World, because you did lots of good things in your earth life. You started to develop your wing muscles there, to sort of 'feather out' for the journey onwards. Those wings were strengthened by working on virtues like love and compassion, fortitude and courage, helpfulness and encouragement, generosity and trust."

Sophie is nodding; she knows about virtues.

Lumina goes on. "Without those virtues, Sophie, our spirit wings are weak when we take off. Then we have a really tough time when we arrive here.

"So, those faint lights, those dim light-bodies you've already noticed—they understand now, and are working on themselves. But, you did good,

Sophie; so here you are, rosy and ready. Your bird-spirit is flying free, and on you go."

"But where the heck am I going?"

# 4 THE QUEST

Lumina draws himself up to his full, awesome height, totally aglow, and addresses his team. “We, the Light Knights, are going on an epic Quest to track how humanity has earned its spiritual wings over eons of time, to see how we humans fit into the cosmic picture. We were given intelligence and a questing spirit for a reason, and we haven’t been left to waft off in all directions either.”

“I bet this is about our GOD connection. Right, Lumina?” Sophie holds up a light-hand, slowing him down. “Remember, I’m pretty new at this, because my parents never really filled me in on GOD. They said they didn’t know where to begin. I sure see their problem now. So, GOD created everything, right? And you’re saying that GOD gave us a curious mind to ask questions and sort of appreciate what GOD has done?”

“That’s it,” says Lumina. “And there’s a powerful element to this relationship—love. It all started with GOD creating a creature that He loved, one that could love Him back.”

“Why do we call GOD a *He*?” asks Sophie.

This question bugs Lumina, too. “GOD isn’t a *He* or a *She*, but we have to use something, and *It* just doesn’t cut it. GOD is way beyond ‘*it-ness*’, isn’t He? Language can be limiting, so bottled up, so .... So, Sophie, will *He* do for you?”

"Ah, no problem," says Sophie, shrugging her light-shoulders. "So ... you were saying that GOD cares about us; there's a kind of personal connection?" Sophie is baffled by the notion that a humungous GOD could care about a little smidgeon like herself.

"Not only that, Sophie, but because we have intelligence and the power to make choices, GOD has been giving us guidance, laws to obey, that help keep us in order. The challenge is that we have to *choose* to keep things in order, *choose* to obey."

Before Sophie can say anything, Eric jumps in again. "Look at it this way, Sophie. The cosmos operates on laws, right? Otherwise there'd be total chaos, stuff just zinging around. Or, there'd probably be nothing at all, no universe, just a black hole, a complete void. But the cosmos does exist. Scientists are continually delving, going deeper and deeper into understanding the governing laws that hold it all together. So, if humanity is a sort of conscious mini-cosmos within that, with minds of our own, then we need to obey laws to create the order that holds us together, so *we* don't end up destroying ourselves. How's that?"

"Whew!" says Sophie, going through the motions of wiping her fevered light-brow, "This is like university, guys! I'm hardly eleven, and I feel like I've entered university! This Light World is incredible! Yeah, right .... Oh, right! Laws!" She remembers the point. "Boy! If there are any laws in that mess of an Earth World, where are they? Come to think of it, there are lots of laws that just don't agree with each other. Who's right, huh? Tell me, guys, how do we know which way to turn?"

Sophie's fired up, and sparks are flying again. Suddenly she squidges to a halt. "Lumina! Are you saying that GOD has a kind of *Grand Plan* in mind, some sort of *spiritual laws* for human order that we need to uncover ... to understand?"

Lumina pulses, swells and swirls through a rainbow of colours, beyond anything Sophie has ever seen before. He comes to a rest again, sparkles still dancing around him.

Sophie has flung her light-arms around Eric. "Lumina, don't scare me like that!"

His laughter rings out, its vibration dancing all around them. "You've hit the nail on the head, Sophie, the whole reason for this Quest!"

She flashes a look at Eric.

He just grins at her. "Sophie, you brilliant creature, you! Our Quest is *exactly that,* to discover GOD's *Plan*—you guessed it! Before we Light Knights zero in on the problems plaguing the Earth World, Lumina's treating us to an epic journey. You and I are going to time-travel with my big bro and find out about this '*Big Plan*', how GOD has worked with us humans, His special conscious creation, since the beginning of time. We can't sort out the Earth World's deep problems until we fully understand what GOD's Plan is all about. *Then* we Light Knights can zero in and help the Earth World find peace."

Sophie eyes them, poised. Now what?

# 5 TIME-TRAVELLING

"Okay, Light Knights," says Lumina, taking charge at last. "If we get separated it can get really tricky, so we'll use a password to keep us in touch, just in case. Like ... how about '*Quest-Ho*'?" Eric and Sophie nod gamely. It has a certain 'ring' to it, like a navigator going off over the horizon ....

"Okay, let's try it out. Sophie, you stay put. Eric and I will zip off somewhere. You put your index light-finger up and say '*Quest-Ho*' to get us back. Okay?"

"Hmmm, I might—"

"Sophie!"

"Okay, okay. Go ... go ... *GO*!"

PPHHhhhSSsssssttTT

And they're gone, really gone. Just like that. Sophie swivels her light-head around, looking all over for them.

"Yikes!" she squeaks. "Ohhhh ... heeeelp!" Her light-body is turning blue with anxiety. "Okay, okay ... calmly now .... Let's do it. So, I put my light-finger up and say ... '*Quest-Ho*'!"

PPHHhhhSSsssssttTT

As suddenly as they left, they returned.

"Well, howdy, Miss Sophie! How y'all doin' today? *Hmmm*?" A mischievous grin splits Eric's light-face.

"Oh, Eric! I've never been so nervous. Don't you *ever* do that again!"

Lumina chuckles. "Okay, Light Knights, listen up! I'm taking you back, way back, to about a million earth-years ago. We're going to drop in on our distant ancestors in the deepest heart of Africa. We're going into the Rift Valley of ancient times, and find out how it all began. It's the vast, warm womb where humanity evolved over the eons, and it stretches for thousands of miles from today's Jordan to far-off Mozambique down south in Africa."

"The Rift Valley? Lumina, why did humanity happen to evolve there?" Eric eyes his brother.

"Apparently the Great Rift Valley had all the requirements to really push our ancestors out of the trees and onto their feet. It was warm, really warm, and very volcanic, with wet and dry seasons. Nature challenged our ancestors. That innate, intelligent, creative GOD-given spirit of our ancestors was challenged to the hilt. We had to figure things out to just survive. Many times over the eons humanity was nearly wiped out, but we were destined to survive and thrive, pure and simple. It was part of GOD's Plan, d'you see?"

Lumina waits, as Eric thoughtfully nods his light-head; all sorts of scenarios buzz around in there.

Sophie is looking and feeling just a little apprehensively blue again. She hasn't tried this time-travel stuff, and isn't too convinced she's going to like it.

"Trust me, Sophie. It'll be okay. I'm 'driving'," says Lumina. They huddle together. "Light-fingers engage!"

Out go the index light-fingers. And ... contact! "*Quest-Ho!*"

PPHHhhhSSsssssttTT

They pop out in a steaming-hot, jungly place, somewhere up in the trees. Life seems to bubble all around them. Wildly glorious birds call noisily and swoop, monkeys chatter and swing around the trio's invisible light-heads, creatures are trumpeting and roaring all over the place. Dinosaurs? No, no. They're extinct now, but elephants are browsing, snakes are slithering, and predators are prowling about.

"Wow! My brother would love this!" shouts Sophie, agog. Her light-head swivels as new sounds of snorting suddenly erupt.

Some hairy men gather around a hulking creature caught in a pit and pinioned by sticks. A rhinoceros? They're so organized, circling, circling, taut with concentration, spears ready, poised. And then the war-cries begin, and they move in, thrusting their spears at the beast.

"Eeeuuuu, gross!" Sophie scrunches her light-eyes shut, ducking her light-head, and she turns a ghastly green. "I don't like this one bit. Get me out of here *now*!"

Lumina pulls her in. Ping! "Sorry, Sophie. They're gone. I just wanted to show you how we early humans teamed up, how we depended on the hunt and on each other to survive. But, it wasn't just about killing for food, you know. Right from the beginning we realized that another life was sacrificed to give *us* life.

"And you want to know something? We were grateful. See the families around those campfires down there? We felt akin to the natural world then, a part of it. We understood that all creatures had spirits, a life force that was precious, a part of it. We felt we were taking in the spirit of the animals when we ate them. Uh-oh! Don't turn green again, Sophie."

"Boy, if I weren't a light-body I'd have real trouble with my stomach right about now!"

Eric grins, turning to Lumina. "But we were afraid of nature, too, weren't we? There was just so much we didn't know, things we couldn't explain. My mind boggles trying to imagine the beginning of communicating, of putting thoughts into words. Necessity must've driven that process, too. We needed that bond. We needed each other."

Eric pauses, and then his light-eyes dance, his light-arms swinging sparks, gesturing at the limitless universe. "And just imagine our ancestors reaching out to the invisible powers that made things happen. There's that bond to GOD! So prayers must've started by asking the 'spirit-powers' for help. And we're creative, so we developed rituals as shields against the frightening unknown. I can see the ceremonial dances, the masks, and costumes ....

"Aha! Just like we needed hunting leaders, we also needed prayer leaders for spiritual protection, didn't we?" Eric eyes his brother.

"Yup. So, let's put this into perspective. From our earliest days, humans were thinking in terms of spirit. No matter how primitive we looked, we were spiritual. We felt aware, felt connected to the cosmos, felt connected somehow to the mystery of life. Does that make sense?"

"Sure," says Eric. "I can imagine looking up at the stars, and wondering what they were, watching the sun move across the sky in the daytime, the moon at night .... And eclipses! Boy, those must've puzzled us." He muses on silently.

Sophie swirls her light-arms around in a flurry of sparks, as though waving a magic wand. "And thunder storms booming, and wild lightning flashes cracking trees, and ferocious floods wrecking our homes and drowning us, not to mention droughts drying up our water, and awful, horrible diseases making us sick, and other scary stuff .... " Her rosiness is turning a bit blue as her light-mind paints vivid pictures. She's doing a good job of scaring *herself*!

Ah, but then she stops, and turns rosy again. A new, happier thought has burst upon her. "Eric! Babies! I mean, look at the miracle of birth. That's such a mystery, too, just seeing new life pop out, like a gift from another invisible world. I can imagine a mom back then saying 'thank you' as she cuddled her baby, praying hard to keep her baby safe from all the scary stuff that could happen anytime, and hurt it .... Can't you?"

The brothers smile as she dilates with love.

"So ... ," Lumina continues, "praying and ritual became the connection, the GOD-bond between us humans and our Creator. And then we learned how to make fires on purpose by rubbing sticks or striking flints together. It was miraculous, like harnessing the power of the sun, or harnessing a bit of GOD ... magical and sacred. We didn't just cook with it! So, fire ceremonies were held for the success of the hunt, for celebrating important events from birth to death—they were seen as a vital connection to GOD, a connection to his approval and protection. And, we sat around those sacred fires and told stories, too, about the puzzles of life and the Mystery behind it all."

Sophie looks very pensive, her rosy light quite calm. Looking down at the families around the fires, she imagines their lives, their stories. She's feeling akin to them. "I feel it, that awe of the unknown, the mystery of the GOD-being behind it all. It's sad to lose that awe, isn't it? I think that's what's wrong with us in the Earth World today; we've forgotten how sacred life is."

Eric and Lumina nod. They couldn't agree more.

# 6 SPIRIT IS THE FIRE

"Hundreds of thousands of earth-years passed by, ice ages came and went, and ancient human populations moved," Lumina continues. "We left the womb of eastern Africa, that awesome, vast Rift Valley, and spread into the continent. We settled the seashores, spilled out to the islands of the ocean, or migrated northwards down the Nile River, the pathway to Asia, Europe and the world.

"With time we settled down on rivers and, as a result, farming evolved. We discovered we could grow crops by harvesting and replanting seeds. What a miracle that must have seemed, right? Planting a little seed and watching it grow? We also discovered how to tame animals, herd sheep and goats for meat and milk, and we could train oxen to do the heavy work. As we became more self-sufficient the hunt began to disappear, taking a huge part of our ancient culture with it."

Lumina stops for a moment to let them digest what he's saying.

"I can feel that drive, Lumina," says Eric, "the sense of adventure, the hope for better things to come, the determination to survive. That's the pioneer spirit pushing our brains to the limit. It goes deep, doesn't it, that ability to adapt?"

Eric's light-brow furrows; he gazes off, following his train of thought.

"Exactly, Eric. That human genius for wondering, questioning, pondering, and solving puzzles has propelled our evolution. Some civilizations were wiped out by ice ages and disasters, but ancient man was unstoppable. Crafts developed, like masonry and stone-carving, pottery, and glass.

"But imagine the intelligence of realizing that there was metal in rocks that could be smelted out, like copper and gold, then tin and iron; that they could be fused into alloys like bronze, shaped in all sorts of ways, especially for tools, and weapons, replacing the old bone, flint and stone."

Sophie suddenly bobs up again. "Lumina, it just occurred to me how incredible language and speech really are. Human minds grew because of words."

"Right on, Sophie! Just imagine how speech evolved!"

"Oh, I can. I bet words started with imitating sounds and pointing, like charades. I can imagine giving names to things. And when people began to *really* communicate, language just mushroomed and took off."

Sophie's brown light-eyes glow. The possibilities are endless. "And think of the thousands of languages that exist now—wow! I wonder how many billions of words exist .... "

"Super-intelligent, right, Sophie? And it won't ever stop. Ideas and knowledge have been shared and passed down from generation to generation since time immemorial. That's how civilization has evolved."

Sophie is still perking away. "And music, Lumina! Like Eric said, it's like the universe is humming! So I think in the Earth World singing makes us feel in tune with the mystery of existence. Hey, chanting and hymns are really like poems connecting us to the mystery. Cool! And I think instruments like drums, flutes and things pick it all up and give it a beat, like a heart-beat. Ooooh, I get it! It's so *spiritual* ...." Sophie wafts off again, flinging little sparks.

Eric has been listening thoughtfully. "Lumina, don't you get the feeling that ideas can come right out of thin air? And what about alphabets? And numbers? It's amazing the way we can take ideas that no one can see and make them visible. Our imagination, our curiosity, our ability to experiment—the sheer genius of it all! That's what humans are all about, isn't it?"

"And Eric, think about this: the heart and spirit of a culture, the beliefs of a people, are given expression through stories and rituals all bound up and tied together with spiritual meaning. And we call this 'religion'. That ancient sacred fire, with its inexplicable energy, seemed to link the human soul to GOD, the Mystery behind all creation. Religion became the essential glue of human civilization, summing up our thinking, offering us positive values, giving meaning to our existence. Does that make sense to you, Sophie?"

"Yeah, I'm really getting the picture, Lumina. We humans have this GOD thing in us that we call our soul. And it wants to be in touch with its Creator. Not only that, but GOD wants to be in touch with us, since He created us in the first place—beautiful!" Sophie is glowing, a lovely rosy-gold.

"Soooo," she goes on, "what we believe is what makes us grow as humans, and our Quest is to find out more about how GOD works with us? Then we'll be able to help the Earth World go in the right direction?"

"You've got it, Sophie." It's all sinking in, and Lumina figures it's time to make tracks.

"Okay, it's time to move on, Light Knights! Now we're off down the Nile to zero in on ancient Egypt, when the pyramids were built."

Lumina grabs Eric's and Sophie's light-fingers. *"Quest-Ho!"*

PPHHhhhSSssssstttTT .... And they're gone again.

# 7 THE MYSTERY OF THE PYRAMIDS

From their world of light the Light Knights emerge again over Africa.

"Look!" Lumina gestures with his light-arm. "Do you see the two rivers rising from those huge lakes in the mountains down there in the middle of Africa? They join to create the Nile. This majestic river flows on northwards through Egypt, like a great snake, until it finally empties into the Mediterranean Sea.

"Can you see that there's desert on all sides? The Nile gave life. Every rainy season it would swell and flood, spreading rich, silty soil over the land on either side, turning its banks green with vegetation. Over the millennia millions of us migrated down the Nile, but some stayed behind and settled in the Valley. As a result, over 5,000 earth-years ago, a wonderful civilization evolved along the Upper and Lower Nile, one ruled by kings called pharaohs."

Sophie nods. She's read about Egyptian kings and stuff like that.

"Hey Lumina! There are the pyramids!" Eric zooms in to have a good look, Sophie hot on his light-trail.

"This is just amazing! I've always been fascinated by these pyramids. Just look at them, Sophie—they're massive! They sit here in the desert guarded by their sphinxes, thousands of years old, and just shout of mystery."

"Sphinxes—that one's huge! It's so cool, with its human head and lion's body!" Sophie darts over to it. "I read somewhere that sphinxes crouch there protecting their pyramids, ready to gobble up any invaders. Hey, why in the world would anybody think of building all these huge and weird things? Where do ideas like that come from?"

"Religion!" exclaims Lumina. "The Egyptians thought of the forces of nature as a whole galaxy of spirits ruling their existence. They gave these spirits names, made them into gods. They built a relationship with them, prayed to them, asked them for help and protection. Their highest GOD was Amon-Ra, symbolized by the Sun—the light and warmth, which is the source of all life.

"Osiris was the temperamental god of the Nile, and Isis, the goddess of Rain. According to legend, Osiris was murdered, but was brought back to life again by the love of his wife, Isis, just like the River Nile dries up into mud in the dry season and comes back to flowing life again with every rainy season. So the Egyptians believed Osiris arose from the dead."

"That's so neat. So, obviously, the Egyptians believed in the whole idea of life after death, eh?"

"You bet they did, Eric. It was central to their beliefs. And that should give you a clue as to why the great pyramids were built by the pharaohs."

"Well … they were rich and powerful, and full of themselves," muses Sophie.

Lumina chuckles. "That's for sure. But don't forget that every civilization has built grand things, symbols of their belief in GOD. The pyramids weren't temples, though. They were tombs for the pharaohs. Any guesses why?"

"Okay, I'll bite," says Eric. "If the Egyptians believed so strongly in the afterlife, they must've spent their earth lives preparing for it, especially the all-powerful pharaohs. And, I always got the impression that the pharaohs thought of themselves as divine, descended from the gods, more powerful than human …. " Lumina nods as Eric continues. "So, did they build the pyramids as palaces for their afterlife?"

"Right on, Eric. The pharaoh was considered a personification of Osiris, so on his death, the pharaoh was embalmed to preserve his body, and servants accompanied him into his tomb bringing bowls, cups and jugs, food and wine, furniture and pillows, all for his comfort in his new life. Great treasures were arranged all around the burial chamber. And then the pyramid was sealed shut."

"But Lumina," Sophie cries out, "those pharaohs were the mummies! You know, all wrapped up in miles of cotton strips, and stuck in boxes. Did they think they were saving their dead bodies for their new life? I mean, their bodies couldn't work anymore, could they? Why would they go to all that trouble? And all that yucky embalming fluid—eeeuuuuu!"

Thrusting up her perturbed light-arms, sparks flying, all sorts of weird pictures blink through her light-mind.

"Whoa there, Sophie," says Lumina. "Just think! Not only the Egyptians, but all humans, all through our history, have explained things we couldn't understand by wrapping them up in symbols, and creating stories and myths to explain their meaning. The mummies were symbols of eternal life, the stories of the gods were myths to explain life, and inside every myth there's a truth. The ancient Egyptians had it right. They believed their spirits went on to a new life."

"So, stories make something that's difficult easier to understand? I get the sneaky feeling that myths are full of meanings," says Sophie.

"That's it, Sophie." Eric is excited. "This is so true. There are layers of meaning in myths, like the skins of an onion you keep peeling off."

Sophie nods happily, and then turns to Lumina. "So Lumina, what's next?"

"Okay, Light Knights, we have some inkling of how humanity has evolved; once we settled down we started getting organized and built cities and awesome things. We know a bit about the ancient religion of Egypt and its myths.

"Now let's zoom over to ancient Mesopotamia, the land between the Tigris and Euphrates Rivers, where Iraq is today. We'll follow the curve of the Fertile Crescent from Egypt all the way over to the Tigris-Euphrates Valley, ending up in the Persian Gulf. Believe me, the story just gets more interesting.

"Hold on! Contact ... *Quest-Ho!*"

PPHHhhhSSssssstttTT

# 8 THE LAND BETWEEN THE RIVERS

Like invisible eagles, they find themselves soaring above the Earth World.

"Look down there!" Lumina points his light-finger. "See those two big rivers flowing south from the mountains in Turkey? The Tigris comes down on the right and the Euphrates on the left. In between is ancient Mesopotamia, which means 'the land between the rivers'. This ancient land was called the 'Cradle of Civilization'. Now we're back about 5,000 earth-years ago."

"But Lumina, I thought Egypt was the cradle. You know? Out of the womb of the Rift Valley and into the cradle," says Sophie.

"Good point, Sophie. But it was in the ancient state of Sumer, in Meso–potamia, that writing was invented, and so recorded history began. These Mesopotamians developed an alphabet that was much more advanced than the Egyptian hieroglyphics on the tombs of the pharaohs. The capital city of Sumer was Ur, down there in the south where the two rivers close in."

They zoom in on all the activity, gazing at the clay brick buildings. It's all so organized, with gardens growing profusely, some festooning rooftops, palms full of dates waving in the sun, while laden camels, and wheeled wagons pulled by oxen plod wearily by.

"Lumina, look at all those irrigation ditches. They turned the desert into gardens."

"Right you are, Eric. These ancient peoples were ingenious. More than 5,000 earth-years ago they tamed the land by irrigation. No civilization could have grown up without water, and they had two big rivers to work with. But the story is more dramatic than that. Before this civilization emerged, a disaster happened. Do you know the Bible story of the Great Flood, Sophie?"

"Of course! Everyone's heard of that! But, it's just a story, right? One of those myths? I mean, how could everyone drown except Noah and his family? And how could Noah find those giraffes and lions and get all those animals on one boat? It had to be a horrible mess on that ark after forty days and nights. Eeeuuuu!" Sophie's light-face scrunches up.

Eric grins broadly at the image, and turns to his brother. "Lumina, this flood reminds me of the Nile flooding. But something more dramatic must've happened. According to Noah's story it rained forty days and forty nights. Well, if it rained so long, then maybe a lake in the mountains up in Turkey, broke through and washed down.

"I'm thinking there were huge lakes of glacier melt left by the last Ice Age, dammed up by rocks and debris in the mountains, that finally overflowed with all that rain, and washed down, burying civilizations with the devastating force of millions of gallons of water and tons of rubble.

It's amazing that anyone lived to tell the tale."

"Yeah, it *was* a miracle, Eric," agrees Lumina. "And this is where the story gets really interesting, because Noah was GOD's Messenger, one of the very first to hear GOD's Voice, and that's why he lived to tell the tale."

"*Messenger*?" Sophie's curiosity is really piqued. Here's another new idea.

"Yes, Messenger! Remember how I said that GOD didn't let us waft off aimlessly in all directions? Well, He sent us Messengers. Now we'll see how GOD reached out to us through his Messengers, and drew us in to Himself, how He gradually unfolded His Big Plan.

"The myth enshrining GOD's Messenger, Noah, goes back well beyond 5,000 earth-years. It has many layers of meaning, but the most important meaning for us was that the boat, the ark, represented the teachings of Noah. His Message was meant to save the souls, not just the bodies, of those who believed in him.

"He came to save a misguided, wicked people from themselves, to show them the true path to GOD—the path to honesty, truthfulness, and fairness. He offered them rules to create a safe world. But only Noah's family listened. And as we well know, the rest perished.

"Noah's story was handed down over the ages by oral tradition, from generation to generation, and belonged to a Semite people, the Hebrews, who lived in Mesopotamia along with the Sumerians. Now hold that thought.

"Are you with me, Sophie?" She nods gamely. "The ancient Sumerians did write down their stories with their cuneiform script, but the civilization died out eventually, and nobody was left who understood the script. Thousands of years later some archeologists figured it all out and finally the *Epic of Gilgamesh* and the flood came to light."

"Gil-ga-mesh?" says Sophie. "Who's he? I thought it was Noah and the flood."

"Gilgamesh was the Sumerian version of the Hebrews' Noah. These two cultures shared the Valley, you see, and they shared the memory of the ancient flood. Gilgamesh's story was almost lost after the Sumerian culture disappeared, but we know about Noah because the Hebrews didn't die out. And they preserved their stories, including the story of Noah, till they were finally written down in the Bible. Only these ancient Hebrews kept track of their history. Can you guess why?"

"GOD! I bet it had something to do with GOD!" Sophie waits expectantly, her light-head cocked.

# 9 THE GOD OF ABRAHAM

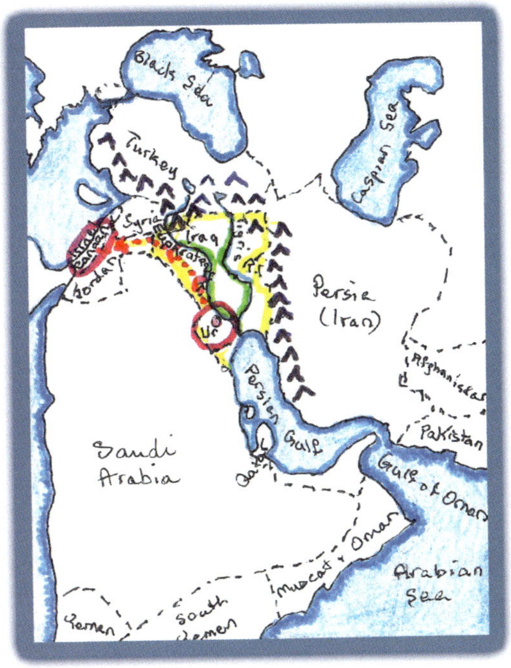


"You bet it did, Sophie!" Lumina just beams at her. "GOD enters the scene big time now. This is the story of Abraham, a Hebrew born about 4,000 earth-years ago in Ur, the capital of Sumer. Up to then the Mesopotamians had seen religion as a way of living in harmony with the forces of nature, like the Egyptians. Then Abraham, the Hebrew, heard GOD's Voice."

"Scary! He must've thought he was going crazy. Did anyone else hear it?"

"No, Sophie, and that's a mystery, too. GOD *chose* Abraham and spoke only to him. He was even called the GOD of Abraham so He couldn't be confused with other gods. You see, like the Egyptians, the Mesopotamian people were praying to gods they'd created themselves, with their own myths and everything."

"So, Lumina," Eric jumps in, "are you saying Abraham made sure the Hebrews got the real story? Was it through him that the beginning of the Bible got handed on? Those stories, like Noah and the flood, must've existed for a long time, even thousands of years, before he came, right?"

"Right, Eric. Abraham made sure the Hebrews who came after him understood that GOD had always planned to be known to humanity, that the Hebrews were the *chosen people* to bring GOD to the world, and Abraham was the one to lead the way. The story of Noah is different from Gilgamesh, you see. The *Epic of Gilgamesh* talks about natural forces, remember, not GOD. But, in the Bible, GOD spoke to Noah, so the Hebrew version sees GOD at work. From the powerful myth of Creation, on through Adam and Eve, and then Noah, and on to Abraham, the Bible is a story with a mission. It's like a dialogue between GOD and His creatures."

"Whoa! That Creation story at the very beginning of the Bible, it says we were made in the image of GOD, right?" asks Eric.

"But Eric! GOD's *invisible*! How can we look like GOD?" pipes up Sophie.

"Look at us, Sophie. We're invisible light-bodies, aren't we? Conscious, thinking souls. That's how we're made in GOD's image, see?"

"Wow, now I get it!" She dances off, delighted with herself.

"Lord, there she goes again! Hey, Sophie, come back here!" calls Eric.

"Lumina," he says, turning to his brother, "I've never really understood that story of Adam and Eve. I mean, ping—Adam appears, and ping—Eve is made out of his rib? And then the snake!"

Sophie is back and all light-ears. Snakes?

"Eric, the Creation story is, first and foremost, a powerful myth. Can you imagine trying to explain to ancient man about cosmic evolution and the evolution of all organic life, including ourselves? The Creation story is absolutely brilliant, using 'days' for huge steps in time, having things appear in a certain order which we now know is completely logical. And, humans were set apart, a step above the natural phenomena, because GOD *breathed* into us, giving us a conscious soul with the ability to think, question, discover, and understand. We know this was to bring us closer to Himself, eh? That soul was created pure and noble, in 'GOD's image' .... It's all there in this myth."

Sophie is listening, and nodding. They have been over this territory already.

"Which brings us to the story of Adam and Eve, and there are many layers of meaning in that myth, too. Adam was really GOD's Messenger, the first we know of, teaching us all how we *awoke* to our destiny as humans. I think the snake acted as a catalyst; it tempted Eve to eat the 'fruit of knowledge' that would change everything. And she wanted Adam to eat it with her. In a way, Eve was the soul, and Adam, the physical body. As a result of eating that fruit, they really became aware of themselves for the first time and realized that GOD exists. Then they had to leave behind their unknowing innocence forever. That's the message. Do you follow?

"Eden represents humanity's babyhood, our nursery. So, Adam and Eve show us how we were forced to go out into the world and take the first steps of growing up. We all had to leave Eden, the babyhood of *not knowing*, and learn to take responsibility for our actions. GOD started humanity on the long, long road of getting to know Him, the road to spiritual maturity, through his Messenger, Adam."

Eric is quietly nodding his light-head. "That makes real sense to me, Lumina."

Sophie has also been following carefully. "It really shows us how special we humans are, doesn't it? How GOD is like a parent, guiding us, making us grow up. I like that way of seeing it. Okay, Lumina, so what about Abraham! We've left Abraham behind."

"Right, so we are back about 4000 earth-years ago, and like the Egyptians, the people of Mesopotamia had their pyramids. See those stepped pyramids down there? They're called *ziggurats*. They tower over the other buildings, but they're temples for worship, not burial. The Sumerians believed that the higher you built the ziggurat, the closer you got to the gods. And they prayed to a huge array of them. They made clay images, idols, of all those gods. They believed that even those clay idols were powerful."

"Hard to imagine how people could see man-made things having all that power," observes Eric.

"Yeah, Eric, and it's interesting that the Hebrews got themselves involved with these things, too. Abraham's father, Terah, actually made those idols. He worked at the Sumerian court of King Nimrod and was immensely important. Then, after Abraham heard the Voice of GOD, he told his father to give up his idol worship. He said clay figures were powerless, that he should recognize the true GOD, the invisible GOD of Power and Good.

"And guess what Abraham did—he smashed those idols! What a shock! It flew in the face of all those people's ideas and beliefs! But, Abraham stood up to them all. He proclaimed that GOD had made a *Covenant* with him, an agreement, just as GOD had made a Covenant with Noah. He explained that just as GOD had told Noah to build an ark to save his people from the flood, now GOD told him, Abraham, to take his people and leave Mesopotamia, to go west to the land of Canaan, and save the Hebrews from the danger of drowning in the sea of idol worship. GOD to the rescue again!"

"Wow!" says Sophie. "It's really spooky, isn't it, Lumina? I mean, only Abraham heard a Voice, and he expected everyone to listen to him, trust him, and just drop everything and go?"

"I think he was terrifically brave, don't you, Sophie?" says Eric. "He put everything on the line, risking ridicule, rage, even violence, for his beliefs. People can be so emotional, eh? Especially about sacred traditions, things one doesn't dare question or change, fearing horrible revenge from those gods ... the Earth World is still full of this problem, not just thousands of years ago! We're still blindly following old, useless traditions. It's at the root of my big question of changing ourselves, isn't it?" Eric is shaking his light-head, really vexed.

"So true, Eric," says Lumina, his light-arm is across his brother's light-shoulders, "but, back to Abraham, folks, and let's see how he did. Those who really knew him, trusted him completely, so they followed him. They were convinced that he was GOD's Messenger. They left their homeland of Ur and travelled north to Haran where Abraham had Hebrew friends and family, and there he married Sarah. It was from Haran that he took his followers to Canaan in the west, on the shores of the Mediterranean Sea. They took sheep and cattle with them, ready to set up a new life. He would become revered as the great Patriarch of the Hebrews."

"What's this Covenant you mention, Lumina?" asks Sophie. "The same one GOD made with Adam and Noah? And now Abraham? It sounds *really* important."

"You bet it is, Sophie! This Covenant is a powerful force, the actual agreement between GOD and his human creation. It's the *key* to the whole puzzle we are set on solving, how GOD has worked with us for thousands of years.

"So, Light-Knights, here we go! Next stop is the land of Canaan! Grab hold! Contact ... *Quest-Ho*!"

PPHHhhhSSsssssstttTT

# 10 THE COVENANT

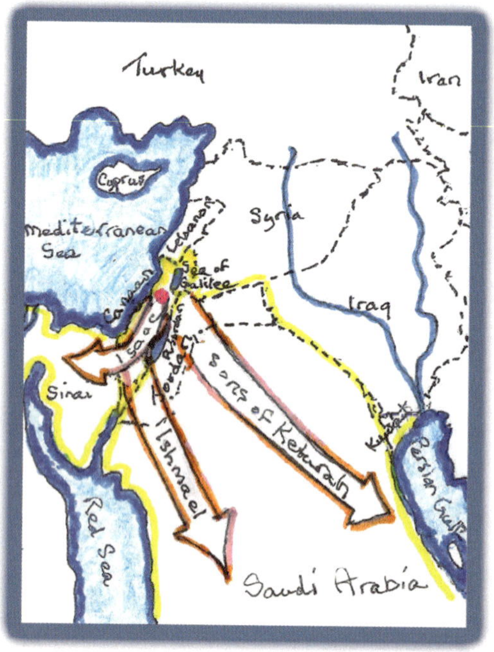


In the blink of an eye they emerge once again, this time into a landscape of water and grass, wildflowers waving in the breeze, little pink and white cyclamen and red anemones ....

"Oh, this looks so peaceful. I love the flowers—is that chamomile? I'm sure I smell chamomile!" Sophie's light wavers longingly. "So is this where Abraham's family went?"

"Yes, Sophie, he found a place to start a new life. But it wasn't easy. He had to move in on other people's territory, you know. However, he and his family prevailed and stayed.

"So, GOD kept speaking to Abraham, and told him to look all around, that all the land in sight, from the Nile in the west and to the Tigris in the east, would belong to his descendants. They would build great nations, they'd be plentiful like 'the dust of the earth'. In the Book of Genesis GOD says, 'By you, all the families of the earth shall be blessed'."[2]

"That must've seemed impossible," remarks Eric. "He didn't have much, did he? Just some sheep and cattle. What about children?"

"Good question, Eric. Abraham had no children. Sarah was barren, couldn't have children. In those days, a wife could give her maid to her husband to have children for her, so she sent Hagar, and Hagar had a boy, Ishmael. The problem was, though, that Hagar got full of herself, quite arrogant, and made Sarah miserable.

"Then a miracle happened. Even though she was really too old to have children, Sarah begged GOD for a child, and she, too, at last had a son, whom she named Isaac. With that, Sarah sent Hagar and Ishmael packing. Be gone!"

"Hagar deserved that! I would've done that too." Sophie is indignant, light-hands firmly planted on her light-hips.

Eric and Lumina grin at each other.

"So now Abraham had two sons to inherit the earth," continues Lumina. "GOD said that each would inherit kingdoms; Isaac would inherit Canaan and all the lands to the west; and Ishmael would inherit the north of Arabia, just to the south of Canaan, and to the east. Time went on, and Sarah died. Abraham re-married. His new wife, Keturah, gave Abraham six more sons. They inherited the southern part of Arabia bordering on the Indian Ocean and the Persian Gulf."

Eric is puzzled. "But Lumina, what is Abraham's Covenant with GOD really about? It's a kind of relationship, isn't it? And did Abraham's children inherit this personal relationship with GOD, along with the land? GOD had a purpose in setting up that relationship, didn't He? Not just to feel cozy with His creation .... GOD talked about the future; He could *see* the future."

"Yes, the GOD of Abraham gives humanity a sense of destiny, Eric, that we aren't just some fluff being blown by the winds of fate, going nowhere in particular, prey to the whims of imagined gods, or our own imaginations for that matter. Do you remember what GOD said to Noah?"

"Lumina, that's the rainbow story!" Sophie chimes in. "GOD said he'd never destroy us again. And the rainbow in the sky was the sign of His promise. Cool! So, is the Covenant a Promise?"

"It is, Sophie, but, we have to keep our end of the bargain, too. Remember the rules we talked about to bring order to the world? GOD promised to guide us, send us help. But we have to obey those GOD-given rules to avoid chaos. No amount of wishful thinking will prevent chaos, only right action will do the trick. The Covenant is like a binding contract, and it protects us as long as we obey. So far, the rules are basically to know that there's one GOD, we're GOD's children made in His image, no idols are permitted, and we must be truthful, honest, and law-abiding.

"Now, we have one more huge assignment before we leave Abraham's people. Light Knights engage ... *Quest-Ho*!"

PPHHhhhSSsssssttTT

# 11 THE STORY OF JOSEPH

Eric, Lumina and Sophie are hovering again over the pyramids in Egypt. This time they can see people crawling around on them, building them. Men are moving gigantic stones up ramps. It's grueling labour.

Suddenly Sophie lets out a yell! "Those poor men are being whipped! They're bleeding. It's awful! How can we let that happen! We've got to do something!" Eric swirls his light-arms around a distraught Sophie to keep her from flying off.

"Hold on, Sophie!" says Lumina. "Our job right now is to try to understand what happened long ago. We're time-travelling, and we cannot change history. Our turn will come in the future. Right now we're back about 3,700 earth-years ago, and the pharaohs are using slaves to build the pyramids. Believe it or not, thousands of them are Hebrews, descendents of Abraham."

Sophie spins around in her column of light. "What? Lumina, we left Abraham in Canaan."

"There's a reason why the Hebrews are here now, Sophie. Remember Abraham and Sarah's son Isaac? Well, he had a son, Jacob, who became known as Israel. Jacob then had twelve sons who became the fathers of the Twelve Tribes of Israel. There was a lot of rivalry between the older sons and the two youngest, Joseph and Benjamin, because Jacob loved his youngest boys the best. They were the sons of Jacob's second wife, his beloved Rachel.

"The story goes that the older brothers plotted to kill Joseph, but Reuben, the oldest, intervened. Instead of killing Joseph outright, they threw him into a pit while they were out in the fields tending their father's flocks. A caravan came along headed for Egypt, and they sold Joseph to the caravan people. Then they took Joseph's coat, the coat that Jacob had given his son especially, covered it with animal blood, and lied to their father that Joseph had died."

"That isn't how GOD expected his Chosen People to behave! That's breaking all the rules!"

"Exactly, Sophie. The story goes on that Joseph was very intelligent and quickly earned a lot of respect in Egypt. The Pharaoh had two dreams that no Egyptian wise man could interpret. Joseph, the Israelite, had earned a reputation for understanding dreams, so he was sent in to the Pharaoh. He explained the dreams, that Egypt would have seven years of good harvests followed by seven years of drought, and that the Pharaoh must save up grain for the coming famine. The Pharaoh was convinced, so he put Joseph in charge of organizing the grain storehouses.

"And it all came true. The drought spread all the way to Canaan. Joseph's father and brothers heard about the supply of grain in Egypt and went to beg for help. The brothers had no idea what had become of Joseph, and their father thought he was dead. Well, Joseph dreamt that his brothers would come and bow down to him, to the brother they'd tried to kill!"

Eric picks up the story. "So, they arrived and begged for grain, eh, Lumina? And Joseph recognized them. What a moment that must've been! He finally told them who he was and they begged for mercy on their hands and knees. He not only showed them mercy, he said that GOD forgave them."

"Right, Eric, but time passed, and Joseph died, the pharaoh who knew Joseph died, and the generations of Egyptian pharaohs after him forgot all about his story. What we are seeing now is about 400 earth-years after Joseph's time. Over the generations, the foreign Israelites were enslaved, and became a very necessary labour force for the Pharaoh."

"Very weird," sighs Sophie. "It doesn't look like GOD's Promise of inheriting the earth is going *anywhere*!"

"That," says Lumina, "is a very interesting comment, Sophie. On the one hand it all looks futile, but on the other, there are now thousands of descendents of Abraham. His children have certainly multiplied and are a force to be reckoned with!" Sophie nods, thinking that one over.

# 12 ENTER MOSES

"On with the story, Light Knights. So, here we are, as I said, about 400 years after Joseph's time. That's about 3,300 earth-years ago. And Sophie, this is where Moses comes into the story."

"Oh, I know the Bible story about Moses! He was the baby in the basket hidden away in the reeds down in the Nile River, right? And the Egyptian princess found him—such a cool story! She heard him crying and rescued him. The princess's maid was actually Moses' mother, and she was really scared for her baby. The princess just loved that baby, so she adopted him and called him Moses. And she even gave him back to his own mom to nurse!"

"Sophie, remember why he had to be hidden?" asks Lumina. "Why his mother was scared? Because the Pharaoh, the princess's father, was so worried that all those Israelite slaves might rebel and take over, that he ordered all their male babies drowned."

"That's horrible, Lumina!" Sophie's light-ringlets spring out with the shock, and her light-eyes widen.

"It *was* cruel, Sophie," agrees Lumina. "But Moses lived. He grew up in the palace, even had his mother to look after him, and she made sure he knew about his heritage. When he grew up, he left the palace to rejoin his people and raise sheep. He became very wise and thoughtful, and he married and had children. And then ... GOD spoke to him!"

Lumina pauses, expecting a reaction from Sophie, and he gets it!

"You mean GOD came back?" exclaims Sophie, planting her light-hands on her light-hips again. "Where *was* He all those years?"

"GOD didn't go anywhere, Sophie. Most of the Israelites had forgotten about the GOD of Abraham and his Covenant, and had turned their backs on their heritage. That's what happened. *They* went away. They'd adopted the Egyptian religion of making idols and worshipping them, but, Moses heard GOD's Voice in the Burning Bush. Remember the Burning Bush that the fire didn't consume? The sacred fire again ....

"GOD spoke from the fire saying he was the GOD of Abraham, Isaac and Jacob. His instructions to Moses were to save the Israelites, lead them out of Egypt, teach them the Covenant of Abraham once again, and take them back to the Promised Land of Canaan, the 'Holy Land', as it came to be known. Moses was GOD's new Messenger."

"And I bet nobody else heard *that* Voice either!" Sophie mutters to herself.

"There were thousands of Israelite slaves by then," says Eric, "and it was nothing short of miraculous that one man could lead that horde out of Egypt successfully."

"It took some doing," says Lumina. "Moses rallied the Israelites, and his brother Aaron was his spokesman. Moses had a stammer, you see. He told them about their forefathers, rekindled their faith in GOD, and begged the Pharaoh, Rameses ll, to let his people go. The Pharaoh was losing a big workforce, wasn't he? He might have been afraid of the Israelites taking over, but he needed them too."

Eric jumps in. "It's a fantastic story! I *love* this! Moses seemed like such a humble person, but he was given the power and resolve to beg the Pharaoh to let thousands of his people go. He no sooner succeeded, Sophie, than the Pharaoh went back on his word.

"And that's when GOD intervened big time and sent the seven plagues. Man, they were just unreal. The Nile water turned red, frogs erupted and hopped everywhere, billions of flies buzzed and pestered the people and cattle, spreading disease; the cattle got boils and died in the fields."

Eric pauses, watching with amusement as Sophie gawks.

"And then hail the size of golf balls pelted down; huge grasshoppers—locusts, swarmed and devoured the crops voraciously; the sky got really dark and very eerie ... there must've been a volcano going off somewhere. And then the final blow was the death of all those poor Egyptian babies. The plagues killed them too."

Sophie is goggle-eyed and shivery-blue, but Eric continues.

"So, GOD warned the Israelites to put a special mark over their doors, which they did; and their babies were spared. Sophie, that miracle is still celebrated as the annual Feast of Passover. Well, the Pharaoh, in desperation, called Moses to save his own son who was also dying of the plagues. And guess what? Moses saved him.

"So, the Pharaoh knew for sure that he was under attack from the GOD of Moses. All *that* finally drove Pharaoh to his knees, eh, Lumina?"

Lumina nods. "But remember, Eric, the Pharaoh changed his mind *again*. He didn't get it at all. After the Israelites left his capital city of Rameses, he sent his troops after them. They had to cross water, an arm of the Red Sea.

"See the narrows down there? The soldiers were coming, and the sea drew back, just like it does before a tsunami wave hits. The Hebrews crossed safely along a dry 'highway', but then the tidal wave rolled back, and the soldiers were all drowned." Lumina doesn't dare let Sophie witness that!

"Awesome! But, Moses made it," exclaims Sophie, "and all those thousands with him? This GOD stuff is powerful!" says Sophie. "You don't mess with GOD!"

# 13 EXODUS: THE ENDLESS SINAI JOURNEY

"So then reality kicked in," Lumina continues. "The Israelites found themselves in the Sinai Desert. Believe it or not, it took them forty years to cross the Sinai Peninsula between Egypt and Canaan. Forty years! Moses had the biggest operation in history going on. How did Moses organize thousands of people, feed them, shelter them? And remember, in the desert ....

"So they wandered in great loops on the caravan trails from water hole to water hole, staying in different places for years on end. The story is recorded in the Book of Exodus in the Bible. His brother Aaron was again his right-hand man. They had to organize the Israelites like a moving city. It was a huge task."

"Why did Moses let it take so long, Lumina? He must've been getting old!"

"Moses had to teach his people about the Covenant, Sophie, and that's where the Ten Commandments came in. Moses went up into Mount Sinai to ask GOD for help, and GOD spoke. He gave Moses the Ten Commandments, laws to govern spiritual behavior. This was the only way to make the Israelites obey, to weld them together as a people, to renew their Covenant with GOD. When Moses came down out of the mountain, do you know what they were doing?"

"No, but I bet it was bad!"

"Exactly, Sophie! They'd all gone back to making golden calves, idols, to protect themselves. Moses, transformed by the new power vested in him by GOD, was very angry. He gave them the Ten Commandments, proclaimed that GOD was reclaiming His people, and leading them home. But they must be obedient!"

Eric looks at his brother. "You know, Lumina, everyone's heard of those Ten Commandments, but I don't know what they are for sure."

"Well, in a nutshell, Moses said that there's only one supreme invisible GOD; no image or idol can represent Him; you don't swear and use GOD's name disrespectfully; the seventh day of the week, the Sabbath, should be kept free from work to remember GOD; you must obey your parents; you mustn't kill; you must be faithful to your spouse; you mustn't steal, or tell a lie; and you mustn't desire your neighbour's possessions."

"So those are really basic rules to keep society in order, eh?" Eric muses for a moment. "If we obey these rules we can trust each other and work together."

"That's right, Eric. And there were also dietary laws, inheritance laws, rites and rituals, all the rules that were needed at that time. But the Ten Commandments are always relevant in the Earth World, back then, today, and into the future."

"Makes sense," says Eric.

"Back to our story .... Many died over the years, babies were born, and it was a new people that prepared to enter the Promised Land of Canaan. But before they did so, they built a special box, the Ark of the Covenant, to hold the scrolls of the *Torah*, the first five books of the Bible. The *Torah* records Moses' teachings and everything that happened in the Sinai. It was holy, the Word of GOD, His Covenant with His Chosen People. It alone bound the Israelites together."

"Lumina, when did the Israelites start calling themselves Jews?"

"Good question, Eric. Remember, their ancestor Jacob was called Israel, so the land he lived in was called the Land of Israel. He had those twelve sons, and the whole of Israel was divided up between them. The term Jew refers to his son, Judah, and eventually part of the land of Canaan was known as Judea. Actually, it was Moses who became known as the 'Father of the Jews'. So, when the Israelites arrived back in Canaan, a new chapter began in the saga of GOD's Covenant with Abraham's descendants, the Jews."

Sophie is quiet, thoughtful. "We take so much for granted, don't we, Eric? When we just listen to the stories, we think everything was easy. But it was really, really hard, wasn't it? It seems like remembering and living the Covenant was never easy. We keep veering off, shifting away, forgetting .... Lessons have to be learned over and over again."

"And, Lumina," Eric adds, "I remember Moses died before they even got to Canaan. He could see the Promised Land, but he couldn't reach it.

"But before he died, he made a Promise, didn't he? That someone like him would come one day. Someone who'd say only what GOD told him to say. Moses said that when he comes, the people should heed him. He got across the idea that God would always guide his people; the Covenant would continue. So they had to keep believing in that guidance. He'd done all he could, and now it was up to them."

Lumina nods. "He led his people home, Eric. They came back to Canaan.

"But now, Light Knights, we're off on a completely new path! We're taking a break from Abraham's people and heading north to Aryan country, the wide open pastures of the Asian steppes, the land between the Black and Caspian Seas, just north of today's Iran. And there, around the same time that Moses was leading the Israelites home, out of what seemed like nowhere, another of GOD's special Messengers appeared."

"Cool! What was his name?" asks Sophie.

"Zoroaster," says Lumina.

"Ooooo, his name sounds magical and wizardy, like Merlin or something!" says Sophie.

Lumina chuckles and grabs their light-fingers. "We're off. *Quest-Ho!*"

PPHHhhhSSsssssttTT

# 14 ZOROASTER

"These are the vast plains of Asia, Light Knights, about 3,200 earth-years ago."

"Whew! Lumina, this time-travelling is making me dizzy."

Sophie staggers a bit, and shakes her light-body, making sparks fly. Then she gazes off to the sweeping vistas of dry grasslands and mountains. Dust devils swirl upwards in their eddies of wind. Horses gallop about carrying men and children who ride bareback, dipping and whacking expertly at leathery balls with sticks, sending them flying. Polo?

Eric is keen to hear more about this new Messenger. "Lumina, you say the next step is the story of Zoroaster? Our mum used to talk about him. She said that nobody realized how important he was. She said she stumbled upon him doing research for her thesis, and nearly exploded with excitement. So, what was so exciting?"

"Eric, before I let that secret out, I have to fill you both in a bit. So much history about Zoroaster has been lost because nobody, except the Hebrew-Israelite- Jews, kept records. Not only that, but the Book that Zoroaster gave the world, the *Zenda Avesta*, was burned over and over again down through the centuries by invading armies who were enemies of his faith. This was particularly harrowing because fire was a sacred part of Zoroaster's religion. *Ahura Mazda*, the Great Lord GOD, was symbolized by fire."

"There's that mystical fire again! It seems to be part of each chapter somehow," says Eric.

"Like Moses and the Burning Bush, huh, Lumina?"

"That's it, Sophie. So now we have Zoroaster appearing. The heart of his teachings was handed on through the Zoroastrian priests, the *magi*."

Eric's light-head shoots up. "Magi? Hey, they were the wise men, the ones who came to the baby Jesus!"

"Right, Eric! But you're getting a bit ahead of our story again. We'll come back to the three wise men later.

"So, Zoroaster was an Aryan, not a Semite like Abraham. They belonged to different peoples. About 3,500 earth-years ago the Aryan tribes were on the move in northern Eurasia. Some flowed southwest into Greece; some south towards Persia, today's Iran; and others flowed eastwards into the Indus Valley, today's Pakistan. Zoroaster's people settled north of Persia. They were a pastoral people, with herds of sheep, goats and horses. The Aryans loved and greatly prized their fast horses."

Sophie's still thinking about burning books. "Lumina, why would anyone burn Zoroaster's Book? That's mean!"

"It's usually fear or plain ignorance that leads to destruction, isn't it, Sophie? Remember how stubborn the Israelites were? You said yourself that they were always breaking the rules. So because we have the power of choice, or free will, we seem to have a constant battle inside ourselves."

"I get it, Lumina! Every kid knows what it's like to want to do exactly what he's told *not* to do! My mom used to say that we have to build a conscience, a little voice inside our heads that warns us."

"Exactly, Sophie. You could call it an internal battle of Good—which is GOD—against Evil, like Satan, the Devil, or whatever you want to label it. That's exactly what Zoroaster taught. He talked about the force of light against the force of darkness, and said that human nature has two sides. The dark side represents spiritual ignorance, which produces greed, lying, hatred and war. And the light side is all about spiritual knowledge. You know ... things like love, order, justice and peace."

Sophie pounces. "Back to the virtues again! Yup, we learned all about them in school. 'Virtues, virtues, virtues: the building blocks of character.' Oh, of course! Virtues give us *light*. Cool! You said it! We talked about that - the more the virtues become part of us, the more our light turns up—zap-zap!" Sophie flings out rosy sparks. "Zoroaster really put his finger on that, Lumina."

"He sure did, Sophie. Those who didn't believe in Zoroaster were prisoners of their dark side; their light was really dim, and they tried to destroy him.

"So, he and his followers were forced to move south into northern Persia to make a new beginning. Like Abraham having to leave Mesopotamia to go to Canaan, just to be free to worship GOD, and like Moses leaving Egypt—"

"Hey, Lumina," Eric breaks in, "it was the battle of good against evil that was at the heart of Zoroaster's teachings, wasn't it!"

"Definitely, Eric. He taught that GOD is supreme, that following His guidance puts order into human affairs. This understanding was essential for the salvation of the world, and Zoroaster was really interested in saving the world. The King of Persia was so impressed that he became a Zoroastrian, a follower of Zoroaster."

"Lumina, can we call Zoroaster a Messenger, like Abraham and Moses?" asks Eric.

"That's exactly what he was. Instead of telling people that GOD spoke to him, though, he explained that he found enlightenment from Ahura Mazda, the Great Lord. Just another way of saying the same thing."

"But, Lumina, why did our Mum get so excited about him?"

"Aha! Eric, Zoroaster was the very first Messenger to mention a World Saviour. Up to now we've followed the story of the Jews, and the Promise GOD made to Abraham to bless his descendents. And now here's Zoroaster, off by himself in northern Persia saying that the world would one day be blessed by one of *his* descendents. A Saviour, the *Shah Bahram*, would come from his own family, he said, away off in the future. And this Saviour would bring peace to a very troubled world by fighting the forces of evil, chaining them up for a thousand years.

"He foretold this about 3,200 earth-years ago, a long time before it appears in the Bible—the story of chaining up evil and ushering in world peace. I think that's what excited our mum, Eric. She could see a real mystery there. She wondered if the ancestral lines of Zoroaster and Abraham actually converge somehow."

"Hmmm," says Sophie. "So GOD made a Covenant with Zoroaster, too. The Covenant is spreading out. Does our Quest follow that Promise, too?" She eyes him, poised and expectant.

"You bet!" Lumina beams.

"Woohoo!" Sophie crows. "Where are we off to now?"

"Fasten your light-belts, Light Knights. We're off to find Krishna. *Quest-Ho!*"

PPHHhhhSSsssssstttTT

# 15 ENTER KRISHNA

They emerge once again from their light cocoon into a new vista, with Lumina in the lead.

"Sophie, we're flying down the Indus River Valley that's in today's Pakistan, to the east of Zoroaster's homeland. Remember that the Aryans from the north and west migrated here? That was about 3,500 earth-years ago.

"An ancient Indian people lived here before they arrived. They were very dark-skinned and had a special culture of their own. The paler Aryans charged in with their horses and took over. Those native people who weren't wiped out became slaves, and all their possessions were taken from them."

Sophie glowers as Lumina continues.

"The Aryans who settled in the Indus Valley divided their people into classes. This is really important to understand. The priests, Brahmins, were in the top class. They controlled the spiritual and ritual life of the people. Next came the warrior and ruler class, then the farmer and business class, and finally the lowest, the servant class. Over the generations these class divisions became rigid, and became known as castes. People were born into a caste and could not deviate from the strict rules governing each one.

"But, the conquered people didn't fit into this exclusive Aryan class system, so they were considered outcasts. They were called 'untouchable', and a whole new caste of slaves was born. The untouchables did the really dirty jobs."

"Of all the mean, unfair things to do!" Sophie blurts out, red sparks flying. "Everything was taken from them! Just horrible .... "

"That's an evil of war, Sophie. The winner takes all. So, the Aryan caste system hardened over the centuries into a kind of social 'straight jacket'. You couldn't deviate *ever* from the place you were born into in society.

"The *Vedas* were the sacred texts of the Indian Aryans—hymns of praise to their gods, and the rituals and ordinances necessary for gaining their gods' protection. The Vedas taught that all existence is based on laws, a cosmic order, and that human order is a part of this divine plan.

"The sacred fire was central to their faith too. Offerings were made by their priests through intricate fire rituals to all the powers they believed controlled nature and humanity. That idea sounds familiar, doesn't it?

"Then, out of the midst of it all, about 2,700 earth-years ago, came a new Voice—Krishna. He claimed to be GOD's Avatar, his Messenger."

"Oh—an Avatar! I saw a cool movie once called *Avatar.* But that Avatar wasn't really human. Actually, the gorgeous effects in that movie remind me of the Light World .... " Sophie gazes off, remembering, and then suddenly snaps back. "Hey, was that Avatar, Krishna, talking about the same GOD as Abraham? And Zoroaster? What did Krishna call GOD?"

Lumina nods at Sophie, sorting her questions out. "These Messengers are all talking about the same things in different ways, Sophie, ways that their people could understand. Every culture has its own pattern, and Truth is always understood within one's own pattern. Do you see that? Krishna teaches that *Brahma* is the all-powerful GOD, and the creative power of GOD is called *Vishnu*. So, Krishna said that he was an incarnation—an Avatar—of Vishnu."

"Uhhh, what's an 'in-car-na-tion'?" asks Sophie.

Eric chimes in. "I think that means something invisible being given a physical form, Sophie."

"You mean like us, Eric? We're invisible souls, light-bodies, but in the Earth World we had earth-bodies."

"That's the idea, Sophie." Lumina nods. "The Messenger, Krishna, was the physical person voicing the Message received through the inspiration of GOD, kind of like a receiving station, see? It was the same for Abraham and Moses, Zoroaster ... all the divine Messengers."

"Yup! I see, I do see, Lumina! Were there other Avatars?"

"Yessir. Krishna said he was one in a loooong line of Avatars, and he promised another would follow him, the *Kalki Avatar*. In the future the whole world would be desperate, he said, wrapped up in wars and discord. Peace and justice would cease to exist anywhere; chaos and misery would prevail. At such a time we should look around for the Kalki Avatar, and he'd be there."

"The Covenant!"

"That's it, Sophie!" says Lumina. "The Promise!"

"Krishna had a book, right?" Eric asks.

"Yes, the *Bhagavad Gita*, the 'Song of the Lord'. So, let's look at what Krishna taught his followers, the Hindus. He said that GOD is love, that this Supreme Force loves His creation, and that they must in turn love Him. Each person has an eternal, unchanging soul, the very centre of his or her being, and this soul is a spark of GOD. He said that to find happiness in the Earth World, one should do the very best job one can within his or her caste, and so grow closer to GOD through selfless service, without any thought of reward. That is the essence of peace, order, and happiness. By doing one's best and being content with one's own place in society, they'd build social stability, bringing the soul closer to GOD."

Eric interrupts. "But Lumina! Don't Hindus believe in *reincarnation*, that we don't just go on to the Light World to continue our spiritual journey towards GOD, but we get sent back over and over to the Earth World in new bodies till we become perfect somehow?"

"Eric, that's where our next Messenger comes in, the Buddha, the Enlightened One. Let's go find out! So, hold on, Light Knights. Contact ... *Quest-Ho!*"

PPHHhhhSSsssssstttTT

# 16 THE BUDDHA

"See those incredible mountains down there? Those are the Himalayas, the 'Roof of the World', the highest mountain range on earth. A mighty river, the Ganges, flows from those ice caps.

"And there it goes, flowing south out of Nepal, heading east through northern India and today's Bangladesh, to finally empty into the Bay of Bengal in the Indian Ocean.

"The Buddha was born around 2,500 earth-years ago in the kingdom of Nepal, high up in the Himalayas. He was a royal prince who knew only the sheltered life of the palace. One day, when he was a grown, married man, he left the palace grounds for the first time, and was shocked to see sick, old, and dying people all around."

"You mean he grew up without ever seeing *real* people?"

"That's right, Sophie. When he saw suffering for the first time, he was so upset that he never returned to his palace. He left the high mountains of Nepal and followed the Ganges River down to Benares in India. He needed time to think and meditate. He sat under a tree. It became known as the *Bodhi* tree, the Tree of Wisdom, because as he meditated and fasted, he had an extraordinary experience. He saw the Truth in a glorious explosion of light and vision. He saw all that had ever been and would ever be. Enlightenment!"

"Lumina, I've heard that the Buddha said there is no GOD," says Eric.

"I think, Eric, that in his wisdom, the Buddha taught about the 'Great Uncreated' and the 'Great Unborn'. Puzzling terms, I know, until we realize that GOD is uncreated and unborn. He transcends all existence. The Buddha had entered the Hindu culture that believed in a galaxy of gods depicted in long epics of heroic deeds. It was a time when there was a ferment of new ideas circulating, speculations about the meaning of life, the soul's nature, and so on. And he seemed to be part of that ferment. The big difference was that the Buddha completely separated himself from the old Vedic tradition of the Hindus. Through his experience of enlightenment, he saw through all that cluttered thinking to the real Truth behind suffering. He made a drastic break."

Eric is thinking out loud. "I think he was very wise .... I really think he avoided any mention of GOD because he knew GOD would be lost in the crowd. Then what he taught would have no effect."

"That's very possible, Eric, because the Buddha understood that life is full of suffering only because of our attachments to worldly desires, to traditions, and dependencies on gods. It's like we're prisoners of our own minds, of what we *think*—"

"So," cuts in Eric, "we should think for ourselves, take off our blinders, and see with our own eyes!"

"That's right, Eric, the Buddha said we could change by freeing our minds, curing our thinking, and choosing a better way to live. The Buddha put it all in our own hands! Instead of being imprisoned in old, outworn traditions, we could choose his clear spiritual principles, his Eightfold Path of spiritual, mental and social healing, and transform ourselves.

"It was a revolution, Eric. The Brahmins, the priests in the top caste, claimed the ancient Vedic teachings were the only truth, that there was no escaping the entrenched caste system. Even Krishna's teachings were understood within this caste system. The Buddha, on the other hand, taught that no one, not even the outcast, was a captive of the caste system."

"Wow! I bet the Brahmins didn't like that!" remarks Sophie.

Eric is scratching his light-head. "Lumina, to go back to my question about reincarnation, wasn't it around the Buddha's time that the idea of reincarnation took hold? Our mum said something about that. Somehow the idea of escaping the caste system became so important that the gurus, spiritual teachers, were speculating about being reborn, that the soul could earn karma, 'brownie points', and earn a better rebirth. Didn't they have this notion that the only way to escape the prison of the lower castes was to be reborn into a higher caste?"

"Yes, and the Brahmin priests actually believed that they, the male Brahmins, were the only ones who could escape the constant cycle of rebirth and fly free in the heavenly realm of Nirvana when they died."

"What!" Sophie jumps in. "There were millions and millions of people, and you say that there were four castes, and all sorts of outcasts … and half of them would've been women! And we women couldn't escape rebirth at *all*?" Sophie thrusts her light-hands up in disbelief.

Eric nimbly dodges her indignation. "Lumina, the Buddha was trying to shift the minds of the people, wasn't he? If they obeyed him they would totally change the society they lived in."

"Right, Eric! He taught us to have compassion for all living creatures, put his teachings into action in every facet of our lives, so that our inner essence would change from moment to moment, never static for a second. He said that in the space of an earth life our essence can evolve and change completely, that spiritual growth is true rebirth. No caste system could control that. Do you see? It was like taking chains off the soul."

Sophie is mulling this over. "Like us light-bodies, huh? We're changing; at least I know *I* am, because from moment to moment I feel like I understand more, like my energy is growing. So my light must be getting brighter!"

The brothers grin knowingly at each other. "Sophie, you bet it is!"

Lumina picks up the thread again. "Over the following centuries, opposition and pressure became so fierce that the Buddhist monks and nuns, thousands of them, decided to leave India. But, before we look at that, let's see if the Buddha made a Promise."

"I bet he did!" blurts Sophie.

"You bet right, Sophie!"

"Ooooh, this gets more interesting all the time! What a cool pattern … over and over again … like a treasure hunt! I'm loving this Quest!"

"It just gets more and more interesting, Sophie! The Buddha said there were Enlightened Ones before him, and there'd be another after him, away off in the future. He'd be the *Maitreya Buddha*, the Buddha of World Fellowship, and this Buddha would bring peace to the world."

"So Lumina," says Sophie, "this Promise sounds the same, only in different words! Zoroaster said *his* descendant would chain up evil and create peace. Then Krishna said that when all was in chaos *he* would return and create peace. And now the Buddha is saying *he'll* come back and bring fellowship and, *again* … world peace. Are they all talking about the same future Messenger? Are all these Messengers connected somehow? Like GOD working through a series of links in a spiritual chain?"

# 17 THE GREAT SILK ROAD

Lumina throws his light-arm around Sophie's light-shoulders, giving her a squeeze. "It's all getting more and more fascinating, isn't it, Sophie? You really see a pattern emerging now, don't you? Still game?"

Eric and Sophie nod and gaze at him, just waiting.

"Okay, Light Knights, let's take a bird's-eye view of the known world about 2,500 earth-years ago. The Buddha came at a really extraordinary time in human history. By then Zoroaster's teachings of the coming World Saviour had been spread far and wide through Persian conquests and wars, affecting the whole Mediterranean area. At the same time, there arose great teachers from ancient Greece, like Plato, Aristotle and Socrates. Their writings were permeated with wisdom. They dreamt of an ideal world reflecting the same hope for peace in the future.

"And remember the land of Canaan, the Holy Land? Well, there, the Jews were under the siege of waves of invasion. And the great Jewish prophets, like Daniel, Isaiah, Jeremiah, Ezekiel, and Hosea, were exhorting the Jews to remain faithful to the GOD of Abraham. They said a deliverer, a *Messiah*, the one promised by Moses, was coming. Their description of this Messiah, though, sounded more like the prophesized future Zoroastrian Shah Bahram, and not at all like a man resembling Moses. This Messiah would chain up evil for a thousand years and restore GOD's kingdom!"

"Sounds like an explosion of expectancy and hope all around the Mediterranean Sea," remarks Eric.

Lumina nods, but Sophie shakes her light-head vehemently.

"Lumina, we're talking about 2500 years ago. That's ages ago, and we still have so much distrust and war. Where did all that hope go?" Sophie is looking up at them both.

"It's coming, Sophie, but we're still putting all the building blocks in place, and now, Light Knights, we're going to have a look at China.

"You see, at the same time as the Jewish prophets, Greek thinkers, and the Buddha were so busy, great teachers arose in China—Confucius and Lao-tzu. Confucius spoke of social order, very classified like the Hindus. And Lao-tzu taught about spiritual balance or 'going with the flow', a natural rhythm in harmony with the elements of nature; through spiritual balance one could achieve peace within. It was Lao-tzu who gave us the *yin-yang* idea of interwoven opposites in life, the complementarity of light and darkness, male and female, and so on."

"Oh, *yin-yang*!" Sophie laughs. "My mom used to say to Dad that he was so *yang*, so typically male!"

Eric grins at her. "And you, Sophie, are very *yin*, very feminine, eh?"

"Okay, you two." Lumina gives them a nudge. "What I want to do now is expand the scene. There were sea routes for trade all around the Mediterranean world, and caravan routes from the Mediterranean coast all the way to India, but nothing connected these land routes to China yet. The humungous, impenetrable Himalaya Mountains acted as a barrier."

Lumina zooms them in over an awesome panorama of mountains and deserts.

"Then a very clever Chinese traveller found a pass through to the west, about 2,100 earth-years ago—that's 400 years after the time of the Buddha. His name was Chang Ch'ien. The story goes that he set off westwards from Sian, a big trading centre and seat of government in central China. Nobody really knows why he did this."

Sophie bobs up. "Oh, I know why! That's easy. He was just plain curious. Somebody, someday, was going to want to go over those mountains to see the world on the other side, huh, Eric?"

Eric nods. "But imagine how persistent he must've been, Sophie. I mean, see that country down there? Those are the highest mountains on earth, the 'Roof of the World'. And look at those huge deserts to cross, too. Chang Ch'ien must've hooked up to caravans, travelled from oasis to oasis, braved the desert heat and cold, listened to stories .... Something drove him, some inner push. There goes that human pioneer spirit again. It makes me think of the climbers who have braved Mount Everest and lived to tell the tale. Of course, Chang Ch'ien didn't try *that*. But I marvel at him finding any way at all."

Lumina agrees. "You've got the picture, Eric. It was a tortuous, punishing route. However, Chang Ch'ien was ingenious and determined. He worked his way through those mountains, trading his way along. He brought goods with him, his own little caravan."

"So, that's how he survived!" says Sophie. "He was a real trader. He knew how to buy his way along. Clever, very clever ... and just imagine how he felt when he popped out on the other side—'woohoo'! I bet they heard his shout all the way back to Sian!"

Lumina chuckles. "So, what have we got here? If we look at the picture from the western end again, the main caravan trade route ran from the ancient Mediterranean seaports of Tyre in Lebanon and Antioch in Syria, on overland through Judea and Jordan, then to Mesopotamia and Persia, through Afghanistan, where it shot off south to India, and then on east to Chang Chi'en's pass. From there the route continued east along the Chinese trade routes, skirting the Gobi Desert, and travelled hundreds of miles to Sian where it hooked up to other trade routes heading further east again. It was long, thousands of earth-miles long.

"But, listen up, Light Knights! Here comes the punch line that seals the deal. When Chang Ch'ien made his breakthrough, he brought something new and precious to the west—brilliant, shiny Chinese silk. Silk was unheard of in the west, and it was so beautiful that all the kings and rulers had to have it. And the 'Great Silk Road' was born, the longest overland trade route in the world!"

"Silk did all that?"

"It did, Sophie. The Romans, Greeks, Persians, Indians, and Egyptians all wanted this fine, shiny silk. But, the Great Silk Road carried more than trade; it became the highway for new ideas as well. That's how Chinese and Western spiritual thought finally met. And stories of World Saviours, too .... "

"Lumina," says Eric, "I can see how the world's opening up now. So much went on for so long in different pockets of the Earth World, cut off from each other. It just boggles my mind to think of the impact these people had on each other!"

"Eric, after generations of perseverance, when Buddhism was forced out of India to avoid being reabsorbed by the Hindus, the Buddhist monks and nuns migrated along the Great Silk Road to China. Buddhism, with its teachings on spiritual growth, took root and flowered in China. The prophecy regarding Maitreya, the future Buddha, flowed in and throughout Southeast Asia and Korea, and on to Japan, where the Promise of 'world-mending' struck a deep chord. This prophecy became a symbol of hope all the way along."

"Awesome! Hope! So, the Promise is encircling the Earth now. Hope for the future is spreading through the Messengers, isn't it?" Sophie's light-face is agleam. She's not so downcast now. There's hope ....

"You've got it, Sophie! The Messengers were like flashing beacons throughout our history. All the Messengers, without exception, gave us new teachings for healing the ills afflicting the world at the times when they appeared. Each of them pierced through all the accumulated, inflexible traditions with a clear remedy of Truth for an ailing world, and freed the human spirit.

"Now let's go back to the Holy Land and meet Jesus of Nazareth. Remember the Covenant of Abraham? Well, Jesus was his descendent through Isaac and Jacob. Are you ready?" They fuse light-fingers. "Engage ... *Quest-Ho!*"

PPHHhhhSSsssssttTT

# 18 JESUS APPEARS

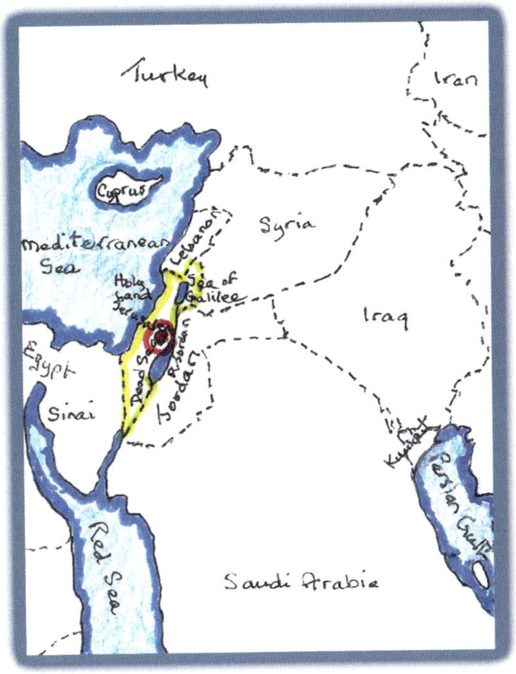


The trio emerges once more from their cocoon of light. “Here we are back in Judea, Abraham’s ancient Canaan, about 2,000 earth-years ago.”

“Who’s that down there in the desert? He’s really excited about something!”

“That’s John the Baptist, Sophie, ‘the voice crying in the wilderness’. He’s calling the people of Israel to mend their ways and return to GOD, because the ‘Promised One’ is coming, ‘one whose sandals he is not worthy to carry’. He wants his people to purify themselves, to be baptised in the River Jordan, to be ready for the Promised One.

“These were momentous times in Judea, because after all kinds of invasions and captivities, the Romans had conquered them and ruled with an iron fist. The Jews were really suffering and feeling rebellious. They were anxiously looking for a Saviour who would free them. John is telling them the time is near, that this Saviour is coming.”

Sophie's light-eye is drawn to a glow in the river. "Lumina, look at that wonderful flash of light—over there, in the River Jordan. What's going on?"

"That's John talking to Jesus of Nazareth. Jesus has come to him to be baptized, but John is telling Jesus that Jesus should baptize *him*. John believes Jesus is the Promised One!"

Lumina zooms them out. "What happened after this was pretty amazing," Lumina explains. "In a moment of revelation, Jesus heard GOD's Voice saying he was the 'Chosen One', the one promised by Moses."

Eric is remembering the story. "Jesus was a simple man, wasn't he? Just like Moses said he'd be. And wasn't John arrested for stirring things up, Lumina? There was so much unrest, so much fear. I remember that the Romans crushed any resistance."

"Yes, Eric. Remember, Jesus went off into the wilderness for forty days to meditate and prepare himself, because he knew the danger he would be facing as people gathered to hear him speak. After that, he began travelling by foot up and down the shores of the Sea of Galilee, teaching anyone who'd listen to him that the Kingdom of GOD was at hand.

"People were so thirsty for hope. He healed the sick and weary with his words and his touch. He taught us to love GOD as GOD loves us, to love our neighbours as ourselves, even to love our enemies. He said we must forgive each other just as GOD forgives us. He taught that love and forgiveness can completely change the world, and that only by turning to GOD can we heal the world. Those who believe in GOD, who are humble and yearn to be good, who are kind and pure of heart—they are the ones who will enter the Kingdom of GOD.

"People flocked to hear his powerful, healing words of hope. And that drew the attention and reaction of the Jewish clergy."

Lumina pauses, giving the others a chance to respond.

"But, if Jesus taught that GOD loves us, where's the harm?" Eric asks the obvious question.

"Jesus called the priests hypocrites, Eric, because they preached one thing and did another. They let the traders and money-lenders into the Temple, and Jesus was so furious that he turned their tables over. He told them to give Caesar what was due to Caesar, and to GOD what was due to GOD, and not mix the two.

"He crossed another line, too, because he didn't stop teaching on the Sabbath. According to the Ten Commandments, it was absolutely forbidden to work on the Sabbath, a day set aside for prayer and meditation. Jesus said he was doing the work of his 'Father', GOD.

"He told the people not to fear those who could kill the body, but fear those who could kill the soul. And he was pointing a finger straight at the clergy. He hadn't come to bring peace, but the sword, the sword of Truth, he said. He'd come not to break the Law of Moses, but to fulfill it; he was the New Covenant as foretold by the prophet Jeremiah."

Eric sees the problem. "So, Jesus was really fighting against two enemies, wasn't he? On the one hand the Romans were afraid of Jewish mobs and insurrection, so Jesus' talk of a 'kingdom' was causing a real stir there. And on the other hand, the clergy quickly recognized that Jesus was leading a spiritual revolution, one that would have a huge impact on their own power. The Jewish people had always looked up to the clergy, and now they would look at them with new eyes, wouldn't they?"

Sophie is nodding as she listens to the two of them, following the building tension.

"Hey Lumina," Eric suddenly exclaims. "I just remembered the three magi, the wise men who came to see Jesus when he was born? They were

Zoroastrians, weren't they?" Sophie swirls around.

"Right, Eric, the three Zoroastrian magi came from the east because they'd seen an unusual star shining in the sky in the quadrant of the 'House of Israel'. They were great astronomers and believed the star was an omen foretelling things happening in the human world. Zoroaster's religion dominated the Mediterranean at the time of Jesus' birth, remember, with its prophecy of the coming of a World Saviour, the Shah Bahram. The question is, if the magi thought Jesus was the Shah Bahram, how could Jesus be descended from Zoroaster?" Lumina smiles quizzically at them. "We'll come back to that mystery later!"

Sophie is struggling to follow the two brothers, still thinking about Jesus and the crowds. "I don't know much about stars and things, but I know that Jesus is heading for trouble."

Lumina nods, zooming them into the midst of a turbulent mob, with fighting and shouting all around them, and stones flying past their invisible light-heads. Roman soldiers wade in, clobbering left and right with their heavy sabers until the people flee for their lives. Sophie bolts to Eric and Lumina's side, her light-eyes popping.

"Yikes! Lumina, get me out of here!" She ducks her light-head instinctively as another rock sails by. Ping—Lumina has brought them back to a calm zone again. Sophie is still quivering.

"Not pleasant, right, Sophie?" says Lumina. "Those mobs are dangerous, nobody knowing what's right or what's wrong, just lots of thoughtless anger and confusion. Doesn't it remind you of mobs you've seen on television in the Earth World?

"So, in the midst of it all Jesus was arrested and put on trial by Pontius Pilate, the Roman governor of Judea. He was cross-examined, and they tried to trick him into saying he was plotting to overthrow the Romans.

But Jesus said he was not a king of the Earth World; his kingdom was GOD's Kingdom, the world of the spirit. Of course, the priests considered this heretical thinking, against the laws of Moses—they thought. Jesus had tried to teach them, tried to make them understand that he had come to fulfill Moses' promise to lead the Jewish people back to GOD, free them from the fetters of this world, like the Buddha, but it was useless.

"In the end, Pontius Pilate washed his hands of the whole affair. He gave the mobs a choice: they could free either Jesus or a criminal who was also on trial, their choice. Well, they chose to free the criminal."

Sophie shuts her light-eyes as waves of sorrow wrack her light-body. "None of those people understood. They weren't thinking at all." Eric encircles her with his light-arms as Lumina goes on with the sad story.

"Jesus was crucified on the cross with two thieves, one on each side. As they suffered that terrible, lingering death hanging there on their crosses, the thieves saw something special in Jesus; he told them that if they believed in him, he would see them that day in Paradise. And then," says Lumina quietly, "they died."

Sophie's light-body is quivering, purply with sadness. "It's all so wrong ... so horribly wrong .... "

Eric's light-arms continue to calm her down as he turns to his brother. "Lumina, before he died, did Jesus make any Promise for the future?"

"Yes, Eric," Lumina says quietly. "He told his disciples that he'd return."

Gathering her wits, Sophie pulls herself together, determined to see all this through to the end. Lumina continues.

"He said that there were many things he couldn't tell them yet, because the time wasn't right, but in the future, the 'Spirit of Truth' would come, and *he* would tell them those things. The Jewish prophet Isaiah talked about two Messiahs. One was the 'sacrificial lamb'[3]—we know that was Jesus. And then later would come the 'Spirit of Truth', the 'Wonderful Counsellor, Mighty GOD, Everlasting Father, Prince of Peace', and on his shoulders would be the 'government' that would bring about everlasting peace.[4] Jesus said that when he returned, the Kingdom of GOD would be established not only in our hearts, but in the actual world."

"Now *that* sounds more like the Zoroastrian Shah Bahram," declares Eric.

Sophie rallies from her bewildered state. "The Covenant! Oh, Lumina, I forgot about the Covenant! No matter how bad it gets, there's always the feeling of hope, isn't there?

"If I have this straight, we're saying Jesus himself fulfills Abraham's and Moses' Promise of the New Covenant? So, when Jesus comes back, will *that* be the World Saviour promised by Zoroaster? So, the three magi were a little ahead of themselves?"

Eric and Lumina grin at each other.

"Good going, Sophie! The three wise men saw signs in the stars of Jesus' coming, but there's much more to come about the Shah Bahram."

"What's going to happen next? Jesus died on that horrible cross, and I get the feeling he was so alone. Did the priests win after all? How could Christianity exist today if there wasn't anyone left to believe in him? How could the Promise come true?"

# 19 A MIRACLE

"You're absolutely right, Sophie. Jesus' companions, the twelve disciples, were heartbroken when he died, and thought it was all for nothing. They completely lost their way. It was Judas, one of the disciples, who handed him over to the Romans in the first place. He sold Jesus out for a handful of silver." Sophie's light-eyes widen. How could he do that?

Lumina continues. "He did! A real traitor, he was, just like Joseph's brothers, jealous and blind. But then an extraordinary thing happened. After his death, Jesus appeared to them! He broke through from the Light World and just amazed them, blew them right away. Then, off the disciples went with the good news, that Jesus Christ would be with them always. He was the 'Risen Lord'!"

"That's a miracle!" exclaims Sophie. "But why is Jesus called 'Christ'?"

"I wondered about that, too, so, I found out," says Eric. "*Cristos* is a Greek word meaning 'anointed', or 'chosen'. It was Jesus' disciple Simon Peter who first called him the Christ, and it meant that he recognized Jesus as the Chosen One, the fulfillment of the prophecies.

"Those who believed in him became known as Christians. The early Christians were the first to understand that if they believed in Jesus Christ, their spirits would never die; they'd go on into the next world, this Light World, and be with Jesus. In fact, his spirit was with them even in the Earth World. What do you think, Lumina?"

"Yes, Eric. Although all the Messengers are with us forever, Jesus was the first to make that very clear. He showed the connection between the Light World and the Earth World, that we are linked to the next world, this Light World, through faith, even while we are in the Earth World. As we gain faith we awaken, our light-bodies burst into real life, and we enter the Kingdom of GOD Jesus speaks of, which is lit by the power of faith."

"So this Kingdom of GOD isn't a place, is it? It's a *feeling* we get when we wake up and believe in GOD .... And our spirit moves into a sort of new world of understanding? Is that what it means to have a 'change of heart'? I remember wondering how you could change your heart .... But it feels like my heart *is* changing." Sophie smiles. "I don't even have one now, but that's how it feels."

She turns her light-face up to Lumina. "Does that mean I'm getting nearer to GOD?"

Lumina beams back at her, nodding.

"Ahhh," she sighs contentedly, closing her light-eyes.

"Hey, Lumina," interrupts Eric, on a totally different track, "didn't something terrible happen to the Jewish Temple after Jesus died?"

"You better believe it!" replies Lumina. "When Christ died, the clergy thought their problems were solved. But they were wrong! They were so blind. If they'd listened and understood Jesus' Message, they would have found spiritual peace. And who knows what might have happened then.

"But no .... The riots just got worse. So finally the Romans reacted with force and squashed the insurrection with one master stroke. They destroyed the Jews' sacred Temple of Solomon in Jerusalem, reducing to rubble the very home of the Ark of the Covenant handed down from Moses. The Ark disappeared in all the destruction. Then the Romans followed this up by exiling all the Jews from the ancient land of Abraham, dispersing them out into the world. Total desolation reigned. Along with the Jews went the little Judean Christian community."

"Just like today, isn't it?" remarks Eric. "So much misery and conflict everywhere, people being forced to leave their countries for so many painful reasons."

"So true, Eric .... Christ's disciples, the apostles, now realized his Message wasn't just for them, the Jews. The Covenant of Abraham embraced all humanity, and Christ's followers carried his Message of hope and spiritual salvation to the cities of the Mediterranean. Nearly 400 years after the death of Jesus, the Roman Emperor Constantine adopted Christianity as the official religion for the whole Roman Empire. His mother, Queen Helena, was a devout Christian, and it was through her that the first churches were built on the Christian sites in the Holy Land."

"But, Lumina," says Eric excitedly, "the Romans used to throw the early Christians into the arena to fight the gladiators in the Roman Coliseum! I saw some pretty hairy epic movies about that when I was a kid in the Earth World, and it was awfully bloody. It's incredible that Constantine became a Christian."

"Well, I think his mother had a hand in that, Eric. Everywhere Constantine turned there were divisions in his Empire. He had conquered so many countries and territories, you see. He saw an opportunity to knit it all together under one common religion. Because he was Emperor, he could simply send out a decree, and from then on Christianity became the official faith of the Roman Empire. As it spread, monasteries were built, and the faith flowered as far as Ireland in the west and the Byzantine Empire of Turkey in the east."

"So, what happened next, bro?" asks Eric. "That peace didn't last long before the barbarians broke down the doors of Rome."

"Let's head off to the vast desert sands of Arabia to find out, Light Knights. There, we'll enter the lands inherited by Abraham and Hagar's son Ishmael. Remember how Isaac inherited Canaan, and Ishmael inherited northern Arabia? And Abraham blessed all their descendants, right? Isaac's line produced the kings of Judea, like King Solomon and King David, who were the ancestors of Christ. And now, out of the sandy mists comes Muhammad, a direct descendent of Ishmael.

"Are you with me? Got it all straight?"

"Ooooh! My poor light-head!" Sophie is grinning. "I'm ready for anything! Lead on, 'O Learned Master'!"

# 20 MUHAMMAD THE PROPHET

"Let's move forward in time again, to 1,500 earth-years ago and the caravans and traders of yore. We're heading south from the Holy Land deep into the Arabian Peninsula, a huge boot of land between the Red Sea and the Persian Gulf with its 'sole' against the Indian Ocean—just above the Horn of Africa.

"Hold tight, Light Knights. *Quest-Ho!*"

PPHHhhhSSsssssttTT

They zoom in over a vast desert with a bit of a green fringe. This is Arabia.

"Wow!" says Sophie. "It's so blistering hot ... that sun just blazes."

Caravans of camels cast long, black undulating shadows as they parade across the sand.

"Oooh my gooooosh, have you *ever* seen so much sand? See those huge hills of sand? They just go on and on forever. How can anyone ever figure out how to get to where they're going? There aren't any roads anywhere that I can see." Sophie is completely awestruck.

Eric, equally fascinated, gazes out beside her. "Dad and I used to talk about this sort of thing, Sophie. He's a sailor, and he'd tell me about celestial navigation. It's an ancient science, handed down from generation to generation by sailors who used the sun and the stars to navigate the high seas. The Arabs used the same concepts. They knew which way to go to find their next watering holes, simply navigating an ocean of sand, instead of an ocean of water."

"It's a tough, isolated world, out there in the desert," says Lumina, "and the fiery Arab spirit was molded by that harsh world. Now our story has reached the time of the Prophet Muhammad. I know there's a lot going on in the Earth World right now, and he's taking a lot of flack that he doesn't deserve. So, let's go back to Muhammad's time."

Sophie and Eric settle in.

"Muhammad was orphaned as a little boy and brought up by his uncle in Mecca, a very busy city and caravan centre, full of traders from all over the world. He, himself, became a trader, a very honest and respected businessman. He belonged to the powerful *Quraysh* clan of the *Bedouin* tribe, who were all descended from Hagar's son, Ishmael. The clan chieftains were in constant competition and feuds with each other, really fierce in their clan loyalties.

"Although the Bedouins were Ishmael's descendents, many centuries had passed, almost two millennia, since the time of Abraham. They'd forgotten about the GOD of Abraham and had reverted to idol-worship. They clung tenaciously to their traditions."

"Lumina, that reminds me of the Israelites in Egypt, before Moses got his hands on them."

"Yes, Eric, and Muhammad, being an unusually spiritual man, was plagued by moral questions. He was torn between his clan's pagan traditions and what he knew was morally right. He used to go off to a cave in the mountains to think."

"Like the Buddha, leaving home, meditating and thinking about the state of the world ...." muses Sophie.

"Well, Sophie, when he was about forty, not young, Muhammad was up there in his cave when he heard a Voice, just like Moses did. Again and again, he heard this Voice, and finally he shared it all with his wife, Khadijah. Was it the Voice of GOD, or was he going mad? Well, she was convinced it was the Voice of GOD, and that Muhammad had a special mission to fulfill."

"What did that Voice say, Lumina?"

"Sophie, the Voice told him to speak, to teach that there's one GOD, the GOD of Abraham, and that he, Muhammad, was His Messenger. He would go on to teach his followers to believe in the Bible, in the Messages of Moses and Christ."

Eric chimes in. "So, Muhammad was calling them back, bringing them into the light of the Covenant again?"

"You bet he was! He was reminding them of their proud spiritual history. He broke completely with clan traditions, disallowed their idol worship just like Abraham before him, and gave them other rules. He said that charging huge amounts of interest to people who borrowed money was strictly forbidden—something like Christ turning over the money tables in the Temple, right? He taught that GOD loved the poor, and that they must take care of the poor in their midst. And anyone who had a dispute should have a fair hearing and find solutions based on fairness and equity, not simply on the whim and decree of some clan chief.

"Muhammad also gave them rules for marriage, property ownership, and the rights of women—that women should be protected, and that they, also, could own land in their own right, something unheard of before."

"That sure flies in the face of the discrimination against women today in the Muslim world, eh, Lumina?" interjects Eric.

Lumina nods emphatically. "Muhammad taught social justice for all, Eric, that high and low alike, men *and* women, were bound by one moral code. That high and low alike must submit to these moral laws. It was like Moses speaking again, wasn't it? Well, that didn't go down well with the clan leaders. Their power was being challenged, their unquestioned authority undermined, and by this upstart orphan! They reacted like the Brahmins in India when the Buddha challenged the caste system.

"Well, young people were listening to Muhammad, and they liked what they heard. They recognized truth and justice in his Message, and saw new opportunities for themselves in a different kind of society. They flocked to his new faith."

"So, Muhammad had the same mission again of breaking old traditions and bringing GOD back," Sophie notes, "sweeping the slate clean, and starting all over."

"It amazes me," adds Eric, "that it's always one man, just one man, who stands up with that Voice of GOD propelling him, and he turns everyone around. It's like a 180-degree turn, eh? Lumina, I've always thought that spirituality was 'sweetness and light', an inner peace that's cut off from the world. But now I realize so much of what we've been talking about is practical, that spiritual principles need to be grounded in our actions in the world as well."

"Right on, Eric!" says Lumina. "If the needle of our inner compass is pointed towards GOD, 'true north', so to speak, then we can set our sails to the wind with confidence and be carried forward, straight and true, our actions guided by these inner principles, and put them into practice in the world. That's one way of explaining what the Messenger does: he's GOD's Celestial Navigator!

"So, Muhammad taught the virtues of justice, compassion, honesty, generosity, courage, and above all, honour—that obeying GOD's laws was the essence of honour. The Arabs understood honour very well. Now Muhammad directed that virtue to a spiritual path instead of it being mixed up with vanity and feuding. He taught his followers to pray to GOD every day for guidance, strength, and protection, and most importantly, to submit their own desires to GOD's Will, not to their own inclinations. Muhammad taught that GOD knows our inner thoughts as well as our outer deeds, and that at the moment of death, the Day of Judgment, we'll all, without exception, come before GOD and face what our hands have done."

"Muhammad makes it sound plain scary!" exclaims Sophie.

"Well, Sophie, he needed to hit home, didn't he, to put the fear of GOD into these tough desert-dwellers and turn them around. His senior clansmen were getting very angry with him, too. They were plotting to get rid of this trouble-maker in their midst. But then the people of Medina asked Muhammad to come and settle disputes in their city, so off he went.

"Medina is where Muhammad emerged from his own people and was recognized publicly as a Prophet of GOD. He was so successful in Medina that people came in droves to his new faith, which he referred to as Islam, meaning 'submission to GOD'. His followers were called Muslims, and his Book, the *Qur'an*, contains all his teachings.

"Muhammad's utterances were taken down by those who could write, then collected, recited, and memorized by his followers. The population was largely illiterate, but all Arabs prided themselves in memorizing stories and reciting poetry at their desert campfires. The *Qur'an* reads like poetry, flows like a melody in the original Arabic."

"Muhammad was really a man of peace, wasn't he?"

"That's the point, Eric. Not one of the Messengers of GOD has *ever* taught violence. They taught peace and justice. One of Muhammad's most important teachings is 'striving in the path of GOD'. To most Muslims, that means doing our best to bring our wills into sync with GOD's Will, so we can arrive at the Day of Judgment with a clear conscience.

"When Muhammad died, however, instead of his son-in-law 'Alí assuming the leadership of his faith, as many believed he should, the clan elders pushed him aside and took over. They established the *Caliphate*, and literally took up the sword for Islam. It was a time of crusade, conquering the world for Allah, for GOD!"

"It seems to me," says Sophie thoughtfully, "that the Messenger tells us what GOD wants us to do, and we humans mess it up afterwards. All the mess is due to us twisting things around, using that 'sword of truth' Jesus talked about in the wrong way."

Lumina gives her a light-hug. "And Sophie, Muhammad actually taught that the ink of the scholar was more precious than the blood of the martyr. Now that's something to think about, right? So, from the sands of Arabia an idea lit the hearts and minds of the peoples conquered by Islam, and knowledge was accumulated across the span of the Muslim world, from Spain to China. It was all translated and handed on in the

Arabic language. Universities were born, new sciences and the pursuit of the arts flourished, and knowledge expanded.

"Then, gradually, after about 500 years, Islam lost its power. But its spark had lit the west; Christianity resurged after centuries of being cloistered following the fall of Rome, and the Age of the Renaissance flowered in Europe."

Lumina is quite animated by the sweeping picture he conjures up.

"Ooooh, wait a minute, Lumina! Are you saying that religions go through stages? Like, they are born and grow really fast, bring new life to the world, bring beautiful things, and then they kind of wear out? And then a new Messenger comes and it all happens again?"

"Bravo, Sophie!" Lumina grins proudly at her. "You know, when Muhammad came he really expected the Christians and the Jews to understand right away that he was renewing their faiths as well, that they would find peace and renewal under Islam. In the *Qur'an*, GOD says 'We have sent inspiration to thee, and that which we enjoined on Abraham, Moses, and Jesus; namely, that ye should be steadfast in Religion, and make no divisions therein.'[5] But, they didn't see it at all."

"So wars happened and still happen, eh, Lumina?" Eric sighs sadly.

"That's right, Eric. The conflicts mushrooming all over the world right now are signs of the chaos spoken of by Krishna, Zoroaster, and the Buddha. They're a symptom of the 'Time of the End' referred to by the Jewish prophets, and Christ and Muhammad."

Suddenly Sophie's light-head shoots up. "What about the Promise? Did Muhammad make a Promise, Lumina?"

"He certainly did, Sophie! Muhammad said the Spirit of Jesus would return. Muhammad said he, himself, was the last Prophet, the Seal of the Prophets, before the return of this Spirit of Jesus. There'd be two 'blasts of the trumpet'. The first would be a Messenger from his own family, the descendants of Abraham and Ishmael, and then, there'd be a second one; and *that* Messenger would be the 'Promise of All Ages'.

"So, Light Knights, would *he* be the descendent of Zoroaster, as foretold? We're really getting close now!"

"The light at the end of the tunnel!" Sophie feels all tingly.

# 21 WHAT ABOUT THE AMERICAS?

"Lumina, everything we've seen up to now has been happening in the 'Old World'," says Eric thoughtfully. "But, what about the 'New World' of the Americas, and all the original American peoples? Mum was really impressed and intrigued by their beliefs, because they existed ages before Christianity blew in with the European explorers. She said the natives of the Americas should've been the ones teaching *us* and not the other way around."

"Yeah!" pipes up Sophie. "And what about Australia? We did a cool project on the aboriginal people there, and their 'Dreamtime' legends explaining the beginning of the world and humanity. And we learned about the Inuit legends, too. What an awesome teacher we had!"

She pauses to ruminate a moment. "It seems to me that wherever we humans have existed, we had our wonderful myths and stories, huh? That's the GOD spirit at work, isn't it?"

"That's so true, Sophie. And maybe someday we'll get a chance to zoom in on absolutely everybody. But we should get back to Eric's question.

"Let's take a quick look at how we humans arrived in North America. It's really fascinating. Briefly, tens of thousands of years ago most of the very first migrants came from northern Asia over a land bridge that connected Siberia to North America; that bridge is gone now. Some also came by the sea in boats, either hugging the Pacific coast, or crossing by sail, using cloud formations, water movement, tides and currents, as guides—all part of their genius. They could read the signs made by the clouds that hovered over the land beyond the horizon. They also navigated by stars; they understood the movement of the constellations across the sky."

"That's not easy, Lumina! Remember how I mentioned that our dad took celestial navigation courses? He's started three or four times and still hasn't figured it all out. And those ancient navigators didn't have any equipment, sextants and things, did they? It was all inherited lore."

"Eric, the more we learn about our early ancestors, the more respect we have for them. Migrations were often propelled by dire need, sending people in all directions, forcing them to adapt all over again."

"They were fleeing from stuff like earthquakes and volcanoes erupting, and horrible outbreaks of disease."

"That's right, Eric. And the Ice Ages were also powerful agents of change; so were droughts and floods.

"So, the ancient Asians flowed into the Americas, and over the millennia they spread out eastwards into the plains, and southwards, on and on. The same thing happened on the Atlantic coast; European traders crossed the North Atlantic by boat, seeking walrus herds for their ivory tusks. Ivory was very precious and in huge demand in the Old World.

"These traders island-hopped through the icy northern seas, beyond Greenland, even up the St. Lawrence River in Canada and down the eastern seaboard of North America, and continuing south."

Eric jumps in again. "I read in a book once that these 'farfarers' in the north would spend the winters with their cargo in these faraway lands and wait for spring before heading home. They'd build shelters, making walls out of rocks, and then use their overturned boats as roofs. Ingenious, eh?"

"That's so cool, Eric! I really think they were a lot smarter than us." Sophie is developing a real pride in her human ancestors.

"And there's more, Sophie," Lumina continues. "Another part of the puzzle was the Phoenicians of northern Africa, who were famous for sailing beyond the 'Pillars of Hercules', the huge cliffs that guard the Atlantic entrance to the Mediterranean Sea, the Strait of Gibraltar. They were fearless navigators who also used the stars and sailed with the currents and winds across the Atlantic. They island-hopped, too, to the islands and coasts of the Americas, north and south. And all for trade! The grass is always greener on the other side, right? They couldn't resist going a little further. So they brought their knowledge, too. Sort of like the Great Silk Road of the high seas .... "

"You know, Lumina, I get the feeling that these voyages were like the challenge of space travel today. Human ingenuity was always pushing the envelope, wasn't it? Some of us were always more curious, maybe more reckless, looking beyond the horizon, eh? The unknown lured us onwards."

"Exactly! Nothing has ever stopped us, Eric."

"Guys, that's GOD at work! That's our GOD spark, isn't it?"

"Sure is, Sophie! We're an amazing species, aren't we? That spark was inherited; knowledge was handed down. The ancient Americans were basically of the Stone Age, and then along came traders with new ideas, right? So, early American Indians were building civilizations at the same time as in the Old World. Millions of inhabitants lived in the Americas before Columbus ever stumbled onto its shores. Many peoples were inland, isolated from the coasts; others were touched by the ideas of invading traders from the seas.

"Shall we explore the ancient Americas a little? Hang on, Light Knights. Here we go! Light-fingers contact ... *Quest-Ho!*"

PPHHhhhSSsssssstttTT

# 22 DEGANAWIDA

"Ooooh, this is gorgeous! The sunset shining on the water, and those birches all pink .... And see those reflections? Where are we, Lumina?"

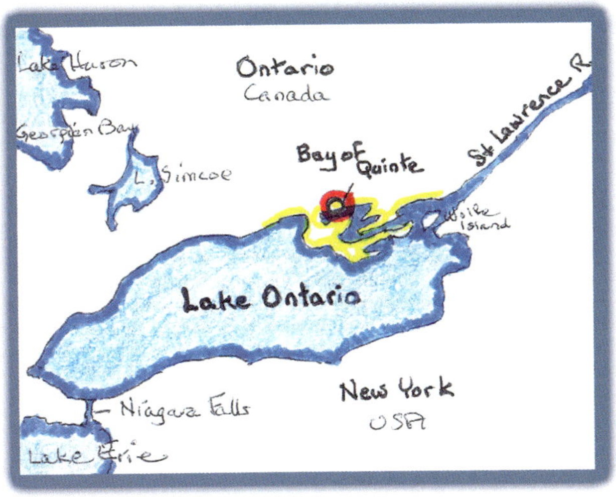


"We're on the shore of Lake Ontario, Sophie, one of the Great Lakes in Canada. Right here it's the Bay of Quinte, the country of the Iroquois Indians before the arrival of the white settlers. Glorious, isn't it? No industrial smog, just clean air and bird-song. This land was sacred to the Iroquois; they depended on it and treasured it."

"It's like there's magic in the air! I feel peaceful ... joyful. I think I understand how they must've felt." Sophie wafts about, a happy pink, enchanted by the beauty around her.

Eric gets down to business, eyeing his brother. "What did they believe in, Lumina?"

"There were thousands of different Indian tribes in the Americas at this time, all with their own beliefs. But in general, the northern American tribes, like the Iroquois, understood that GOD is one eternal Great Spirit, invisible and all-knowing. The human soul, being part of the divine creation, as they believed, means that our word of honour is sacred, so we should never lie. Committing murder is forbidden. It's essential to honour our parents; be clean in body, thinking and action; never steal or be greedy, but instead think of the helpless first. And any surplus should be shared at the great feasts. We must live our lives in the Earth World in harmony. And because the human soul is eternal, we should prepare calmly for the long journey to our ancestors in the heavenly world beyond. Through prayer and fasting we ready our souls."

"This is just amazing, Lumina," remarks Eric. "These beliefs sure sound a lot like Buddhism, or Judaism, or Christianity. There's such a similarity in it all, isn't there? Like some spiritual virus running through all of them! Actually, I don't know why I'm so surprised if there's really one GOD behind our spiritual evolution, eh?"

"He's got the whole world in his hands," sings Sophie, as she wafts off again.

"The American Indians had legends and prophets, too, didn't they, Lumina?"

"You bet, Eric. GOD has never left any part of His human family in the dark. He's been in touch with all of us, right from our earliest beginnings. Remember, GOD has a Plan; He's preparing us for something. So of course the American Indians had prophecies and spiritual guidance, too.

"There's a wonderful prophecy of Deganawida, a revered leader and spiritual Messenger of the Iroquois nation. Hiawatha was Deganawida's disciple."

"I didn't know he was so important!" Sophie sighs, "I love that *Hiawatha* poem: 'By the shores of Gitchi Gumee .... ' Hey! *This* is the land of Gitchi Gumee!" And off she waltzes again, happily humming as she flings her light-arms, whirling sparks.

Eric grins. "Come back, Sophie! Story-time!"

Sophie darts back to their luminous huddle.

"Before Deganawida died here in the Bay of Quinte—"

"Hey," Eric cuts in excitedly, "I just realized something. This isn't far from where I used to live in the Earth World. These amazing things didn't just happen in some exotic place over the ocean. Sometimes they were going on in our own back yard! And, it has just dawned on me that every spot on Earth is someone's backyard. Every important thing we have talked about happened in *someone's* backyard .... "

Lumina smiles. "You are so right, Eric. But, we don't necessarily understand better just because something important happens in our own backyard, eh? We can be too close. Okay, you two, here comes a neat Iroquois legend.

"Before he died, Deganawida had a vision that the Indian people would go through a period of terrible oppression. A time would come when they'd distrust their elders and be invaded by a great White Serpent that they'd befriend. But then the White Serpent would try to choke the life out of them. This White Serpent was the arrival of the White Man.

"A Red Serpent would then come from the north and terrify the White Serpent, which would let the Indians go. And then the Indian people would fall helpless to the ground. A great battle would follow, very dramatic, and an Indian boy would watch. He'd tell his people to hold fast to their own beliefs.

"The Red Serpent would pull a hair from the White Serpent's head and then journey southwards only to be caught by a Black Serpent. The Black Serpent would hightail it north and enter the fray. He'd beat the White Serpent, and look around and see the Indian boy, but he wouldn't touch him.

"Then the Black Serpent would turn to the east and be blinded by a great White Light coming from over the water, from the east, and make a beeline for the sea and swim away to the south, while the Red Serpent would drag himself off to the north.

"Those White, Red and Black Serpents represent the materialistic and destructive forces that would cripple the Indian people, but only for a time. Deganawida said *he* would be that Light from the east, that he'd come back, and his spirit would at last prevail. The Indian nation would then become greater than ever before."

Sophie is just a wee bit befuddled by this, sorting out the serpents, trying to assign roles to each of them .... "Whew, Lumina! I see why you told us to pay attention, but the bottom line is that the story is so full of hope. Good! Wars are so useless! If I had anything to do with it, there'd be no more wars!" Sophie's light-body quivers.

"Hey," she exclaims suddenly, "Deganawida said he'd come back! The Promise again .... "

Eric has been busy thinking. "But Lumina, what about the Incas of Peru, or the Mayans, Aztecs, Toltecs? And all the other peoples of Mexico and South America? They sure had their beliefs, too. Didn't the mighty Aztecs have an ancient stone calendar that makes amazing predictions of things in the future? Lots of people have been talking about that. Wasn't 2012 supposed to be 'zero hour'?"

"To find the answer to that, we need to time-travel some more, Eric," says Lumina. "So, let's go visit the Mayan civilization. That'll take us to the Yucatan Peninsula, south of the Aztec Valley of Mexico, and this time we're going back about 1,000 earth-years. Engage, Light Knights … *Quest-Ho!*"

PPHHhhhSSsssssstttTT

# 23 QUETZACOATL

"Eeeuuuu, it's steaming here! And it's so wet and buggy!" Sophie is flailing her light-arms. They've landed in a swamp. "How can anyone bear it? These nasty flies would carry me away if I weren't a light-body!"

"Sophie, this is the Yucatan Peninsula. Difficult terrain was useful for protection from the tribal competition and wars that were normal here. The Valley of Mexico to the north is a very fertile area tucked into a dry desert terrain. That's where Mexico City is today."

Lumina signals to Eric to stick close to Sophie. His story is about to get graphic.

"A thousand years ago that Valley was the centre of an amazing Aztec civilization, a very bloody one, though, Sophie. They lived in fear that the sun would stop coming up. So, every single day, to ensure the sun's return, they offered up human hearts on top of their temple pyramids. They raided their neighbours and inflicted terrible suffering. It was barbaric. And, the stench of their pyramids was terrible."

Predictably, Sophie reacts in a swirl of purple anger. She's like a volcano spouting sparks. "Ugh! I just can't imagine *any* people acting like *that!*" Eric sticks by her. Sophie is realizing just how depraved humans become when they do not turn to GOD, but turn to their dark side instead. Wars are like that, mindless brutality acted out over and over. Lord! What a roller-coaster ride for her.

"They were a superstitious lot, Sophie," Lumina doggedly continues. "Their civilization was in decline and GOD was definitely forgotten. The Maya, on the other hand, were more civilized. They were here in the Yucatan Peninsula. It may be swampy, but there are no rivers, so the Maya worked out big rainwater reservoirs, and drained off the swamps to make farmland.

"See how organized it all is? We're in Palenque, a city of thousands of inhabitants." Before them are broad avenues lined with buildings.

"Hey, I see a huge pyramid, Eric—over there! What are pyramids doing here? This isn't Egypt or Mesopotamia!" Sophie, putting her trauma behind her, zooms closer.

"Good question, Sophie," replies Lumina. "And the one you see is really significant; it's called the 'Pyramid of the Inscriptions'. A great king, Pacal, was buried inside it, in a stone tomb. Like the Egyptians, right? The stone lid on his tomb is inscribed with intriguing designs that tell the spiritual story of the Maya people and predict the future as well, just like the famous Aztec calendar."

"Lumina, it fascinates me that these pyramids keep popping up in different places," remarks Eric. "There must be some human urge to climb up to the heavens. We always seem to be reaching up, reaching for the stars."

"You've put your finger on it, Eric. The Maya studied the stars. They used the same calendar as the Aztecs, and that calendar was organized according to the predictable movement of the constellations across the sky."

"We humans have always looked up, reached out, wondered why. That GOD spark again .... Feel it, Sophie?" Eric's light-body glows a shining yellow. Sophie nods quietly. She looks out over the city, over the pyramid, over the Earth World, out to space and beyond. She feels the wonder.

Lumina nudges her, brings her back, and picks up the thread again. "The pyramids of the ancient Aztecs and Mayan people are intriguing. They were both temples and tombs. And they were configured according to the positions of constellations, especially Pleiades—very complex.

"Quetzacoatl was their famous spiritual Messenger from over the ocean. He had a mysterious beard, unlike the native Indians, who apparently had no facial hair. His symbol was the feathered serpent. He gave spiritual laws and brought peace and justice to his people. Like the Buddha, he could see into the distant past as well as the distant future."

"Does Que—Quetza .... "

"Quetzacoatl, Sophie."

"Right! Will *he* come back?"

"He did promise to return. Centuries later, in 1511, the bearded navigator, Hernan Cortez, landed with his shiploads of Spaniards at one of the precise times and places where Quetzacoatl was expected to return, according to their prophecies. So the bearded Cortez was eagerly greeted.

"To their sorrow, conquest and destruction was what they received, not exactly spiritual enlightenment. What the Spanish conquerors really wanted was gold. But they did bring Christianity in their wake. That should have meant spiritual enlightenment, but in their ignorance of Mayan prophecy, the Christian priests considered the Mayan people to be savages, so they destroyed their beliefs and their historical lore, replacing it all with Christian beliefs."

"The same thing that happened to all the Indians! Blind, blind, blind! How awful to take away something so precious! Like cutting a plant off from its roots .... Didn't they know they could've built the Christian story on the Mayan people's beliefs, rather than just destroy them; then their history would have been part of the story too?" Sophie gazes off, sadly.

"That sounds suspiciously like what happened to Zoroaster's Book, too."

"Exactly, Eric. Well, luckily a few scholar-priests were more enlightened. They were deeply interested in the stories they heard, and recognized the native wisdom and knowledge, so they interviewed the wise men of the tribes and wrote down what they learned from them before the knowledge died with them. Their records were really important and are still being used by anthropologists today.

"The Maya have an enduring belief, even now, that the true Quetzacoatl, like the White Light of the Iroquois Indians, will return again from the east. The Promise is alive and well, Light Knights!"

"What about that stone calendar?"

"Right, Eric, the stone calendar .... Now *this* is a very interesting calendar. There were five Cycles of the sun depicted on the Aztec calendar and also in the Maya holy book, the *Popal Vuh*, the book of the past, present and future. This mysterious 'book' is the story illustrated on the stone lid of the Maya Emperor Pacal's tomb. I mentioned that earlier.

"The first Cycle of the Sun, eons ago, ended in a deluge; the second Cycle ended in hurricanes; the third, in a rain of fire; the fourth, in starvation following another rain of fire. So, now, Light Knights, the fifth Cycle of the Sun just ended in December, 2012. The Aztec and Maya calendars foretold that this would mark the 'end of the world' as we have known it and the beginning of a pivotal change, a spiritual awakening in the world."

"Whoa! That's now!" Eric chimes in. "That gives us something to think about, eh, Sophie?"

"What's going to happen, Lumina? Can you tell us?" Sophie's light-eyes are flashing in anticipation.

"Not *yet*," says Lumina. "So, the *Popal Vuh* illustrates the birth and history of humanity and prophesizes its future. It's based on the stars and big sun flares that govern the onset of drastic climate changes, and these ancient seers and astronomers mapped it all out. We've seen this gift of vision and wisdom repeated throughout the entire history of humanity, especially from the Messengers of GOD. Amazing, right? It's that GOD spark again."

"Lumina, I get the feeling there are events *really* looming .... I mean, what about other dates religions are waiting for?" asks Eric.

"Aha! The Bible prophecies do pinpoint a date, especially in Isaiah and the Book of Daniel. It's been deciphered to mean that the Second Coming of the Messiah, the 'Prince of Peace', would be in 1844 on the calendar we're used to. The *Qur'an* talks about the year 1260 on the Muslim calendar—the exact same year! That's when the Spirit of Jesus would return, according to their prophecies. The Shia Muslims believe that the *Mahdi*, a descendent of Muhammad, will come to usher in the 'Promise of All Ages', just like John the Baptist did for Jesus. Then a new era of peace and justice will be initiated."

"But, nothing *happened*!" laments Sophie.

"*Aha*!" says Lumina with a grin. "That's where you're wrong, Sophie! In fact, a great deal happened." He eyes his Light Knights, his golden light-body seems to swell, and he goes on.

"We are returning to Persia, to the ancient land of Zoroaster. Just like I promised! Remember how Zoroaster said that one of his descendants would be the World Saviour, the Shah Bahram? Well, Light Knights, that drama is about to play out for us. We'll soon find out what happened in 1844!"

"Oooh, Eric, I don't know if I'm ready for this .... " Sophie's light-body squidges up in anticipation.

"No mercy now, Sophie! We're off to Shiraz, in the once-great land of Persia. Light Knights, engage ... *Quest-Ho*!"

PPHHhhhSSsssssstttTT

# 24 THE BÁB

Through the swirl of light, Sophie, Eric and Lumina emerge into a glowing, fiery sunset that bathes the city of Shiraz in all its glory. It's time for the call to prayer, and across the city the *muezzins* are calling to the faithful from minarets that gleam in the rosy light. A medley of so many voices, haunting and strangely harmonic, age-old and compelling, rings out to the faithful of Muhammad to drop their tools and kneel in prayer.

"Light Knights," says Lumina in a hushed voice, "it's May the 22nd, 1844, and we're at the city gates of Shiraz, in southern Persia. Do you see that young man leaving his friends? That's Mullá Husayn, and he's walking towards that person over there." Lumina gestures towards a man, who seems radiant, glowing with a mysterious light.

"Oooh, who *is* he?" Sophie cranes her light-neck, following the two men.

"Sophie, Mullá Husayn has been on a Quest, much like ours. He's been looking for the divine Messenger foretold in the scriptures of Islam. He and his friends believe the time is at hand for the coming of the Herald of the Promised One, the first 'Trumpet Blast'. They have the expectation that not one, but two, Messengers will appear imminently, remember? Their wise men have had dreams; they've been following the signs. And now, like us, they've been led to the gates of Shiraz."

"Why Persia?" Eric asks Lumina. "Don't the Jews expect the Promised One in the Holy Land? And the Christians, too? And wouldn't Buddhists and Hindus figure he should come to India? And most Muslims probably think he'll come to Arabia again."

"Well, Light Knights, the Biblical prophecies of Isaiah, Jeremiah, Ezekiel, Daniel, St. Matthew, St. John the Divine in the Book of Revelation, and others, spell out the signs and times, foretelling that the Promised One will come from east of the Holy Land. The Hindu and Buddhist scriptures talk of the Kalki Avatar and Maitreya Buddha coming from west of India. And Persia, or Iran today, is right in the middle, between the Holy Land and India.

"Persia, in 1844, was totally overwhelmed by the corruption of the court of its king, Muhammad Sháh, who held the power of life and death in his hands. His greedy princelings ruled all parts of society, and many of the Muslim clergy were caught up in the mesh of their intrigues and scheming. The masses were kept ignorant and miserable under their control, desperate for a hero to rescue them from their suffering."

"Something like the time of Christ, eh, Lumina," says Eric, "when the Jews were all under the heel of Rome and the narrow-minded clergy?"

"Even worse," replies Lumina, "because here it wasn't a foreign power grinding them down to submission; it was their own king.

"So, let's go back to Mullá Husayn. He has met this person wearing a green turban—that is the colour worn only by direct descendants of the Prophet Muhammad. And remember, Muhammad was a direct descendent of Ishmael, Abraham's son. The man with the green turban introduced himself as Siyyid 'Alí Muhammad, and invited Mullá Husayn into his home for tea. Over their tea Mullá Husayn explained his quest, why he was in Shiraz, and *then* ... Mullá Husayn received the shock of his life. Siyyid 'Alí Muhammad, after carefully listening, calmly stated that his quest had been fulfilled, that he was the very one Mullá Husayn was searching for."

"Oh my gosh!"

"Just try to picture it, Sophie. They talked all night, and Siyyid 'Alí Muhammad answered all of Mullá Husayn's questions, before he even asked them. Imagine how blown away he was!

"At dawn, Mullá Husayn emerged, dazed and spiritually on fire. But he had been ordered not to tell another living soul about his discovery, not yet. Not until, like Mullá Husayn, seventeen others found Siyyid 'Alí Muhammad on their own.

"The eighteen who did discover Siyyid 'Alí Muhammad were called the 'Eighteen Letters of the Living'. Siyyid 'Alí Muhammad became known by his followers as the 'Báb', the 'Gate' in Arabic. The Báb said it was the 'New Day of GOD'. He had come to awaken Persia to the coming of the 'Promise of All Ages'—"

"The Promise of All Ages?" blurts out Sophie excitedly. The column of light around her is spiraling rainbow colours. "Is this the one promised by all the Messengers of the past?"

Light-eyes twinkling, Lumina nods very affirmatively.

"Oh-oh!" Sophie goes silent for a moment, trying to take in this momentous news. "The excitement's building up, isn't it Lumina? So he was like a herald? Like John the Baptist?"

"Exactly, Sophie, but even more powerful. His teachings started a whole new faith, turning Persia upside-down. His disciples travelled the countryside, exhorting their fellow countrymen: 'Mend your ways! Purify yourselves! Turn to GOD!'

"Hundreds flocked to his banner, and you can just imagine how that affected the Shah and the clergy—it was a battle cry! Persia was in an uproar. Some of their really important leaders were becoming followers of the Báb. The establishment was rocked; it reacted violently. The Báb was arrested and beaten, and many *Bábís*, followers of the Báb, were brutalized and killed. It was all very horrific."

Eric, who knows Sophie is struggling, wraps his light-arms around her. She shivers, slowly shaking her light-head. When will the suffering of people ever end? Why is it so hard to accept good? Accept GOD?

"From his remote prison in the bleak, isolated mountains of northern Persia, where the Báb ended up, he still managed to send out messages guiding the faithful to be pure and steadfast, as they prepared themselves for the Promised One, whom he described as infinitely more powerful than himself. 'He Whom God Shall Make Manifest', the phrase he used for the awaited Messenger, would be coming very soon."

Lumina pauses, readying himself for the next part of the story. "All the attempts to stamp out this new movement were failing. The influence of the Báb was only growing, despite his imprisonment and the brutality his followers were facing. The blood-thirsty Násiri'd-Dín Sháh, who replaced his father Muhammad Sháh in 1848, was desperate to end the furor devouring the country.

"So, on the fateful day of July 9th, in 1850, just six years after revealing to Mullá Husayn that he was the Promised One, the Shah had the youthful Báb taken to a barracks square in the city of Tabriz to be executed. He was charged with heresy, breaking the laws of Islam, just as Christ had been accused of breaking the laws of Moses almost 2,000 years earlier."

Lumina draws his companions close to him and zooms them right into the midst of a mob of thousands, jammed together on the rooftops and ramparts overlooking the barracks square. People rudely jostle, craning their necks to get a better view, their shrill, raucous shouts fill the air.

Then an eerie silence falls like a curtain, as a regiment with seven hundred and fifty muskets marches out and forms ranks. The firing squad has arrived. The young Báb and his youthful disciple Anís are brought out and suspended together by ropes around their chests, up against the barracks wall. The crowd is avid in anticipation.

Eric and Lumina close in around Sophie as the signal is given and a huge volley of musket fire blasts the air. They watch as the acrid smoke clears. No sign of the Báb. Gone! What! There, all alone, stands young Anís, who had begged the Báb to let him die with him.

"They missed!" Sophie turns to Eric and Lumina, stunned, as the scene fades out. Ping!

"Light Knights, they found the Báb in his prison cell finishing a conversation with a companion. When it ended, he stood up, ready to accept his fate. Another regiment had to be found when the shaken commander of the first refused to cooperate. The second regiment fired three times, as before, and this time the young Báb and his disciple perished."

Both Sophie and Eric are mute. Even Lumina falls silent for a moment before continuing the story.

"And then ... a fierce dust storm whipped up, earthquakes rumbled, the sun darkened, and a pall hung over the land."

Sophie stays huddled against her buddies. Eric turns to his brother. "Lumina, this was all so recent."

"That's right, Eric. 1850 wasn't that long ago, was it? We actually have some written accounts. European oriental scholars were drawn to Persia to find out what was happening, and they wrote about what they saw."

Sophie isn't comforted. "The Báb is gone!" she moans, hanging her light-head. "All the joy and hope has just *gone*."

"Sophie, I know. It is and was heart-wrenching. But remember what the Báb told them? That he had come to prepare the way .... He told the Bábís to be steadfast and strong, that the next Messenger was right there among them. But, this story isn't over yet.

"After the Báb was executed, two hot-headed youth, crazy with grief and driven by revenge, tried to shoot Násiri'd-Dín Sháh, and that was the match that lit the keg of dynamite. The Shah was hardly touched by the attack, but he let loose the troops to exterminate the Bábís. They murdered Bábís and their families throughout Persia. They say 20,000 died in the streets of towns and villages across the country—a terrible, frenzied blood bath. No wonder Europeans heard about it and came to investigate!"

Sophie has had it. She rears up, fuming, fiery red, pulsing with distress. "Enough! How can all this horrible suffering keep happening? Where's the Promised One? How can GOD let this happen over and over again? He's *got* to straighten out these crazy people!"

"Hang in there, Sophie. We're off to Tehran, the capital of Persia. Light Knights, engage ... *Quest-Ho!*"

PPHHhhhSSssssstttTT

# 25 BAHÁ'U'LLÁH, THE GLORY OF GOD

The Light Knights emerge into the heart of the city. Before them is a massive, awe-inspiring marble structure, a grand archway, situated right in the middle of a vast circular plaza. Looking beyond, the trio gaze at the foothills of a magnificent range of snow-capped mountains.

"Awesome!" exclaims Sophie, craning her light-neck, mesmerized by the structure. "This reminds me of the pyramids, it's so huge, but it's soooo beautiful, too! Oh, look! We can go right through the middle of it!" Sophie darts around and through, exploring its elegant design.

"This was known as the Sháhyad Tower, the Tower of the Kings, Sophie." explains Lumina. "It was built in 1971 to mark the 2,500th anniversary of the Persian Empire. It's now the symbol of Tehran, the western gateway to the city."

Eric is fascinated by its construction. "Look at all the marble blocks—there must be thousands of them! And how could they design it to hold up the way it does, with a humungous archway running right through it?"

"Eric, it's the age of computers. It's hard to imagine how this building could have gone up and stayed up, without the help of modern technology," explains Lumina.

"Yeah, technology has really exploded, just amazing how fast things are changing …. "

"That's right, Eric. In the last century and a half, science and technology have raced ahead like never before—really, ever since the coming of the Báb.

"But let's return to our story. After the death of the Báb, in 1850, a mysterious and wonderful event occurred here."

Sophie and Eric are all ears.

"In this city lived a follower of the Báb, Mírzá Husayn 'Alí, called Bahá'u'lláh, the 'Glory of God', by the Bábís. He was a nobleman whose father served in the court of Muhammad Sháh and then that of his son. Like so many other Bábís, he was caught up in the storm of persecution following the attempt on Násiri'd-Dín Sháh's life. He was thrown into a horrible dungeon under the streets of Tehran where he was chained together with criminals and fellow Bábís. It was a stinking, black hole, dubbed the notorious 'Black Pit'. Each day some Bábís were taken out to die, no one ever knowing whose turn would be next.

Eric keeps close tabs on Sophie, as her light-eyes widen.

"It was while he was in this pit," Lumina continues, "that Bahá'u'lláh had a wonderful vision. A heavenly maiden appeared in a blinding light. She pointed towards him, calling him the 'Best-Beloved of the worlds', the 'Beauty of God amongst us'.[6]

"He felt a tremendous power washing over him, like a 'mighty torrent'. He then understood that 'He Whom God Shall Make Manifest', the awaited Promised One, was none other than himself."

Lumina lets them quietly drink in the magic of this moment that happened right there in Tehran not so long ago. The light around them seems to expand, morph and glow, light upon light ....

Finally Sophie breaks the silence. "Ahhhh," she breathes. "A heavenly maiden .... I love angels .... I'm glad the Promised One had an angel .... 'Ba-ha-o-llah'," she says, very softly. Sophie's light-eyes close, her light-body quiets and shimmers as though she is saying a little prayer. Then, suddenly, they pop open again. "Did anybody else see her? Her light must've filled that horrible dungeon!"

"No, Sophie, only Bahá'u'lláh saw that vision. The same story again, isn't it? He was the Chosen One, and only he saw the maid of heaven.

"So, he was finally released after four dreadful months, and by then he was a very sick man. He didn't say a word about his experience to anyone, not yet. But when his young son, 'Abbás, who was only eight, saw his poor father, he saw a new light within him. And this boy knew in his heart of hearts just *who* his father was. But, no one else knew.

"The Shah had been pressured by influential people to release Bahá'u'lláh, but he was far from finished with him yet. He decided to exile him from Persia, sending him on a journey through the mountains in the middle of winter to the city of Baghdad."

"That Shah was horribly wicked!" Sophie fumes.

"The story continues, Sophie. Let's zero in on that journey, shall we? "*Quest-Ho!*"

PPHHhhhSSsssssttTT

Poof! Snow blows through their light-bodies, as the high Zagros Mountains between Persia and Iraq come into view. Sophie shudders as she gazes down on the forlorn little caravan of mules and howdahs struggling along the mountain path. Most of the people are on foot.

"Bahá'u'lláh, along with his wife Navváb, young 'Abbás, and his younger sister Bahíyyih, were sent off in January, the worst possible time," explains Lumina. "Násiri'd-Dín Sháh hoped the terrible journey would just kill them. Little Mihdi, who was only two, stayed behind with his great-grandmother for awhile. So, the family and some attendants plodded their way through the snow drifts of those high, frozen mountains.

"Do you see young 'Abbás and Bahíyyih running around down there? They're bartering for food. It was perishingly cold; can you imagine their suffering?"

They zoom out again, and Eric takes up the thread. "But, they made it! Finally, in March, almost three months later, they trudged into Baghdad. There, the air was heavy with the sweet smell of spring blossoms. It was time for Naw-Rúz, the ancient Zoroastrian New Year. They had survived!"

Eric pauses briefly, a quizzical look on his light-face, then decides he has to ask. "Lumina, you haven't told us how Bahá'u'lláh connects to the Covenant. Is *he* descended from Zoroaster?"

Lumina, turning towards his companions, spreads his long light-arms. "Light Knights, the waiting and wondering is over at last! Bahá'u'lláh was descended from Zoroaster through the *Sasaniyan* kings of Persia, and from Abraham through the descendents of his wife Keturah, uniting in his own person lineages from the Semitic and Aryan religions. Zoroaster prophesied that the Shah Bahram would come from Nur in the province of Mazindaran, just north of Tehran, where Zoroaster lived so long ago; and that's exactly where Bahá'u'lláh was born. There's so much more, but the proof is all there for anyone to investigate."

Sophie is flinging her light-arms happily, unable to restrain herself. "Woohoo! GOD has done it! It's all coming together just like He promised!" She dances off in swirl of rainbow colours.

The brothers exchange grins as they watch her. It's a remarkable light show!

"Come on back, Sophie. We have lots to do still." She zooms in, composes herself, eyeing them both expectantly.

"Now Light Knights," remarks Lumina, "think about it. This is all fine, but if Bahá'u'lláh is a lowly prisoner and an exile, how could he possibly chain up Satan for a thousand years, as Zoroaster promised? How would he bless the world as Abraham promised? And what does it mean to have the government of the world resting on his shoulders, as Isaiah foretold? The Hindus believe the Kalki Avatar will establish order and divine justice out of chaos. Maitreya Buddha is expected to usher in a millennium of peace and world fellowship.

"So, tell me: how could Bahá'u'lláh, a penniless, lonely prisoner, ever accomplish these things? Is it 'Mission Impossible'?"

Sophie plants her light-hands on her light-hips and rears up. "I know how he'll do it! GOD will help him! If he's the Glory of GOD, then GOD simply has to help him, right?" Sophie is ablaze!

"Right on, Sophie!" says Lumina. "The Covenant of GOD is a sealed deal. If GOD has purposed this Day to come for humanity, He means business. He didn't set all this in motion for nothing, so, we need to follow Bahá'u'lláh's footsteps and see what he does."

# 26 AWAKENING THE WORLD

"Bahá'u'lláh arrived in Baghdad in the spring of 1853," Lumina continues. "This ancient city was part of the Ottoman Empire, ruled by Sultan 'Abdu'l'-'Azíz, and he and Násiri'd-Dín Sháh were allies. He helped the Shah by keeping Bahá'u'lláh under house arrest. Thousands of Bábís in Persia had been killed, so the Persian government figured the new religion had been pretty much wiped out. What could one man and a few dozen of his companions do way off in Baghdad?

"Aha! But they didn't know, did they? Nobody knew yet who Bahá'u'lláh really was, not even the Bábís. So over the next ten years, he restored their demoralized faith. His fame and influence grew and spread. This fact wasn't lost on his enemies, which provoked the Sultan to act again. He exiled Bahá'u'lláh for a second time, this time to the farthest reaches of Turkey—to Constantinople."

"Light Knights, it's now April 21st, 1863. And just before leaving Baghdad, Bahá'u'lláh, along with some companions, has moved to this island in the Tigris River; they've pitched their tents here."

"The Tigris River!" exclaims Eric. "Lumina, I've just realized that Bahá'u'lláh spent ten years in Mesopotamia—well, what *was* Mesopotamia ages ago—where Abraham first received GOD's Covenant. We've come full circle!"

"Exactly, Eric! And there's a huge reason for this. Do you see that dot down there in the Tigris River?" Lumina swooshes them in, arriving in the midst of abundant, blooming roses. "Bahá'u'lláh called this island 'The Garden of Ridván', 'Paradise'. Any idea why?"

Sophie turns to Lumina, her light shimmering in new glory. "It was here Bahá'u'lláh told his followers who he really was?"

Lumina nods.

She closes her light-eyes, lifts her light-head and wafts off among the roses, revelling in their beauty, and the world-altering moment that happened here.

Eric breaks in. "So, Lumina, GOD made His Covenant with Abraham right here, all those thousands of years ago; He said He'd bless the nations of the world through his descendants. And now, in the very same place, GOD is revealing the 'Promise of All Ages', the fulfillment of His Promise to Abraham? That's unreal! I mean, the Shah and the Sultan had no idea what they were doing, eh? They actually *helped* GOD fulfill His Covenant!" He chuckles, shaking his light-head in disbelief.

"GOD works in truly amazing ways, right, Light Knights? So, let's get back to our story, back to Bahá'u'lláh's friends who had followed him to the island and pitched their tents all around him. They didn't know yet, they were still desperately unhappy that their revered leader, the one who had rebuilt all their hopes, was about to be cruelly taken from them yet again. It was just too much to bear.

"Then, that fateful moment arrived when Bahá'u'lláh at last unlocked his secret. He told them who he was. He was the Promised One, the very one foretold by the Báb. Jubilation reigned! Hallelujah! He exhorted them to go, spread the 'Glad Tidings' far and wide, that GOD's Covenant was at last fulfilled, the power of GOD's Word released into the world anew. A new era had begun. So, Bahá'u'lláh left Baghdad in clouds of glory, not as a mere prisoner going into exile again."

Lumina stops. It is a pivotal moment for the Light Knights. New power is infusing the story.

"Ooooh," breathes Sophie, as he goes on.

"So, Bahá'u'lláh and his entourage arrived in Constantinople, and after a few months they were sent on to Adrianople, which was actually in Europe. It was here that Bahá'u'lláh wrote letters announcing his Mission to the most powerful kings and rulers of the earth at that time, even to Pope Pius IX. Tsar Alexander II of Russia, Sultan 'Abdu'l-'Azíz of the Ottoman Empire, Násiri-d-Dín Sháh of Persia, Kaiser William II of Prussia, Emperor Francis Joseph of Austria, Napoleon III of France, and even Queen Victoria of England—each received a letter from Bahá'u'lláh.

"He exhorted them to turn to him, believe in him, lay down their weapons and seek peace, and see to the welfare of their people. Some laughed in derision—a mere Turkish prisoner telling *them* to obey *him!* But mostly they ignored him. That is, except for Queen Victoria. Bahá'u'lláh commended her alone for promoting the well-being of her people through a democratic parliament. In response to his letter, she said: 'If this is of God, it will endure; if not, it can do no harm.' "[7]

"Well, that's half-baked, if you ask me."

"Sophie, think about it," says Lumina. "Of all the monarchies Bahá'u'lláh addressed, her royal house is the only one that has survived. *Yes!* He prophesied the ignominious fall of Napoleon III who was all-powerful at the time. And then the German Kaiser's ultimate defeat, that the banks of the Rhine would be covered in blood not once, but twice. He predicted the downfall of the despotic Shah and the Sultan, and the demise of the Tsar of Russia.

"They've all been swept off the face of the earth. Why? Because they didn't simply ignore Bahá'u'lláh, a prisoner in exile who claimed divine power; they paid no attention to his Message to alleviate the suffering of their peoples and establish justice and real peace. They missed the boat completely; they missed the Ark!"

"The world's first real chance, through the kings, to find peace and justice, and they blew it, eh, Lumina? So what happened next?"

"Well, Eric, Bahá'u'lláh said that as a result of their heedlessness, all power would be taken from them and put into the hands of the people. And it didn't do the leaders of religion any good, either, to ignore Bahá'u'lláh. Pope Pius IX ended up stripped of his army and political power, shocking him so much that he declared the infallibility of the pope so that his authority could never be questioned again. The Sunni Muslim leaders lost all their power, and Turkey became a secular state.

"The power of all these religious institutions has been diminishing ever since. And the militant religious fundamentalism we see today is the last 'wag of the dog's tail', really, because it's all about power too; it's got nothing to do with the welfare of the people.

"So we can see what Bahá'u'lláh meant when he said that 'the world's equilibrium hath been upset through the vibrating influence of this most great, this new World Order'[8]! Kings and leaders of religion have all but lost their power, while ordinary people are coming together, gaining strength like never before and calling for real change."

"It's so huge, eh, Sophie?" says Eric. "Unrest has invaded every corner of the earth—the worlds of religion, economics, politics. Even families are destabilized. Everything's shaken up. The chaos is happening now. But what replaces this mess?"

"Yes, what?" Sophie focuses her big, brown light-eyes on Lumina.

# 27 THE GROUND RULES OF THE KINGDOM

"Unity, Light Knights, unity! That's what will replace the chaos. The Covenant of GOD has always been about bringing together the whole human race to live in peace and harmony. *Now* we get down to business, the whole reason for Bahá'u'lláh's coming. You see, he came to finally bring the Kingdom of GOD into reality, and that involves the biggest shake-up in history."

Lumina eyes them both; he has their undivided attention!

"Bahá'u'lláh brought new laws, which he called 'the choice wine'[9]. These laws would underlie the peace and tranquility of the world. '... the day is approaching,' he said, 'when We will have rolled up the world and all that is therein, and spread out a new Order in its stead'[10]."

"So, the kings losing their power .... Is that what he meant by rolling up the world?"

"Partly, Sophie. But there are profound things that will have to change for the human race to be really united. Let's look at some of the things he taught, the 'good news' that all his followers have been spreading.

"He said that there's one GOD, the governing Force of all existence, who created us out of love to know and worship Him. There's really only one religion of GOD, the eternal, evolving Covenant between His creation and Himself. And as for us humans, we're a diverse human family, all flowers of one garden, and leaves of one tree. *We* are the inheritors of GOD's Covenant, the Kingdom of GOD—the whole human family, all the nations, just like God told Abraham. Isn't that what our Quest has uncovered over and over again?"

"Lumina, this all makes so much sense! Everything's connected, isn't it?"

Lumina's smile splits his light-face; he's relishing her spiritual growth. "Sophie, Bahá'u'lláh has given us a whole 'ocean' of knowledge to guide us. So, let's look at just a few drops of wisdom in that ocean.

"Eric, you'll like this one. Remember how you talked about thinking for ourselves, how we don't need to be spoon-fed by others? Well, Bahá'u'lláh says we have the GOD-given right to investigate the truth for ourselves and *never* accept old ideas blindly—"

"Right on!" Eric leaps in, as Lumina knew he would. "Yeah, that's really neat! And look at the Earth World: they now have the Internet, Twitter, Facebook ... all sorts of computer stuff happening .... So investigation has no limits anymore."

He muses for a moment, and goes on.

"You know, Lumina, I'm thinking these instruments are at the root of lots of unrest, too, like riots and revolutions in the streets, because people can use their cell phones to text each other and get instant action. I'm not sure if this is democracy, freedom, and unity morphing, or anarchy and lawlessness. It's all so chaotic."

"Chaotic is the word, Eric, but the thing is, most people see no visible, cohesive goal for all of humanity to pursue together yet. The world needs to understand what Bahá'u'lláh is teaching, and use all these instruments to bring humanity together and promote peace.

"And, they say it only takes a shift of attitude in one percent of the population to begin to shift the whole. Now, that's exciting, eh, Light Knights?"

Lumina goes on. "And, Sophie, here's something I think *you'll* love. Bahá'u'lláh said that men and women are equal in God's sight. They're like the two wings of the bird of humanity, and they both need to be equally strong for the bird to fly."

Sophie flings out her 'wings', her light-arms, and sends sparks flying. "*Yeess!* You can see it happening everywhere! We girls are coming out of the woodwork, turning everything upside-down. Well, actually, we're turning everything right-side-up!"

Eric gives her two light-thumbs up on that one. "Women have had a bad rap for ages, eh, Sophie? It's been a man's world for too long. It was just accepted that women were inferior to men. Now that's *history*, isn't it?"

"Right on, Eric," replies Lumina. "Science has proven beyond a doubt that women have the same brain capacity as men, so those old beliefs just aren't grounded in fact.

"Which leads me to another principle of Bahá'u'lláh: he says science and religion must agree, that they are different approaches to the essence of truth. Science is never stagnant, and many of the things that scientists are learning now, with the new physics, call into question old theories, opening up mysteries they never knew existed."

Eric pounces on this. "That's it! You can see science bursting its bonds as scientists realize there's more that underlies scientific principles than just physical realities. And as far as religion goes, the human spirit is boundless, isn't it? Capable of all kinds of growth. It can't be contained in neat boxes and doctrines the way some religions have tried to do things in the past."

"The human spirit *is* boundless, Eric, with the potential to do so much good. And that reminds me of another one of Bahá'u'lláh's teachings—about education. He talked about material and spiritual education. Material education is what we usually think of, like reading, writing, math, history, science, and so on. He said that this kind of education is very important, but it's not enough. We also need spiritual education, the virtues. Only then will ignorance and prejudice be eradicated, and then humanity will really thrive. Divine principles, spiritual virtues, must guide the application of knowledge. Nothing else will work.

"And, Sophie, if parents have to choose between educating a boy or a girl, it must be the girl, because a wise mother will bring up wiser children!"

"Awesome!" Sophie exclaims. "At last we girls are really being empowered, huh? I know that if I were a mom and had the choice, I'd never, *ever*, send my kids off to war. I'd sit all those politicians down till they figured things out. Why should they be allowed to send soldiers off to war to be shot down just because they failed to find a better way? Or send bombs? It's positively *criminal*, I think!" Sophie's light is getting very rosy again.

"I can't argue with that, Sophie," says Lumina. "And here's another interesting principle that just might help those politicians find a better way. Bahá'u'lláh said we need one shared language, taught world-wide, an 'auxiliary' language; one that already exists, or maybe a new one. Everyone would learn that language along with their own mother tongue. That makes complete sense, doesn't it?

"Not only would that help politicians, but all the peoples of the world would actually be able to talk to one another. They'd be able to consult on important things, and they wouldn't need translators. Think of all the problems that could be addressed, not just political, but economic, social .... Think how 'transparent' we would have to become, how honest with each other we'd have to be, because everyone could hear and understand! And when you think about it, every part of human life needs consultation to find solutions. It really is a spiritual goal, the desire to find unity and agreement instead of war."

Eric nods. "Yeah, new rules have to emerge, eh? These days we're starting to see a trend in some businesses that are turning their backs on materialistic, money-grabbing values and turning instead to principles of good service and fairness in dealing with suppliers, employees, and customers. The media are really going after corruption and promoting the idea of transparency in government and business dealings. I think there's a growing awareness that honesty has to come first for good results to follow. Now *that's* an idea whose time has come!

"Sophie, we can watch things changing from our perch in the Light World, you know. We can be part of that positive change."

Sophie's light-ringlets bob up and down, goldy-rose sparks flying. This is just what she was hoping to hear!

"We sure can, Eric," says Lumina. "And Sophie, let's get back to your idea of politicians finding better ways than wars to solve problems. Bahá'u'lláh laid out the need for a parliament composed of the world's wisest leaders, who'd sit and deliberate, consult and act on world affairs, making binding decisions and putting them into force. The UN, the United Nations, is just the beginning of that idea."

"Wow, Lumina! And you say Bahá'u'lláh gave us a whole *ocean* of guidance?" Sophie holds her light-head between her light-hands, overwhelmed as she thinks about all the work that needs to be done. She almost moans ....

"The poor UN is trying so hard, but politicians just keep messing things up, playing games, hiding the truth, and even making things worse instead of looking for solutions. Are they all blind? Can't they open their eyes and see what Bahá'u'lláh is talking about?" She sighs. "Some of those politicians are as bad as the old kings!"

"Not a pretty sight, Sophie, I know," says Lumina. "Turning old systems upside-down isn't a tidy process. Bahá'u'lláh did say that 'Mankind's ordered life hath been revolutionized through the agency of this unique, this wondrous System'[11]. That's exactly what we're seeing, and it's really messy right now.

"Light Knights, we've seen a century and a half of these teachings at work in the world. The fulfillment of the Kingdom of GOD is well underway. This 'wondrous System' that Bahá'u'lláh gave us back in the 19th century is based on spiritual values. He said that GOD's Kingdom, real justice, is built on love, not power.

"This spiritual springtime will rise up from the grass roots, from ordinary people. It will not simply be applied by leaders and world organizations from the top down. In fact, all the organizations on the face of the earth will eventually mirror the will of the people. This profound populist change of heart will have one goal: to achieve peace and unity. The 20th century was all about Bahá'u'lláh's teachings just starting to take hold. Gradually these teachings are radiating outwards.

"But we're getting way ahead of our story, Light Knights. Remember where we left off? In Adrianople? Now let's follow his footsteps to his next and final place of exile."

"And where's that?"

"The Holy Land."

Sophie's eyes are as big as saucers. "Ha! We *are* following the steps of Abraham!"

"Fasten your light-belts, Light Knights. We're off to ancient 'Akká! Engage ... *Quest-Ho!*"

PPHHhhhSSsssssttTT

# 28 THE COVENANT COMES HOME

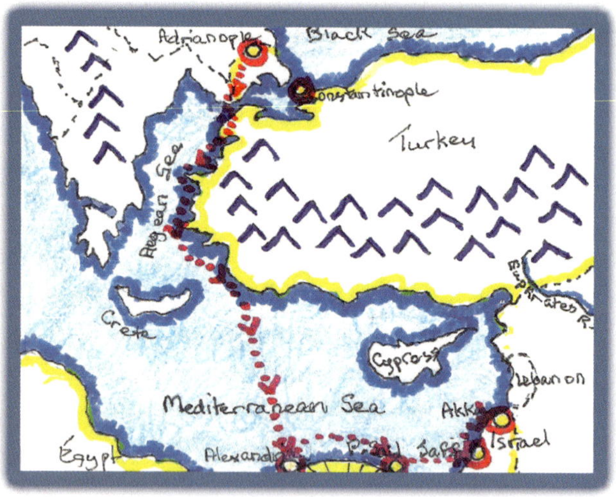


Eric is standing with his light-arms folded, musing as he looks out over the Mediterranean Sea. “Lumina, the Holy Land is such a mystery, isn’t it? Like a spiritual crossroads of the world .... It all started right here with GOD bringing Abraham to the Promised Land, almost 4,000 earth-years ago. Then Moses came back from Egypt, and then Jesus walked the shores of the Galilee 2,000 earth-years ago. I read that Muhammad had a dream that he leaped to heaven on his steed from Temple Mount, where the Temple of Solomon once stood. But the Jews were exiled from the Holy Land 2,000 years ago, and they’re back now. How did that happen?”

“The British put pressure on the Turkish government to issue an *Edict of Toleration* to let the Jews come back. And guess when, Eric?”

Eric and Sophie gaze, expectantly, at Lumina.

"1844!"

"That's the same year the Báb first announced his Message!" says Eric, astonished.

"So, do you think that's a coincidence, you guys?" Sophie's shaking her light-locks, sparks flying. "No way, that's the GOD power at work!"

Lumina and Eric get the message, loud and clear. Sophie is very much with them.

Lumina goes on. "Back to our story, Light Knights. We left Bahá'u'lláh in Adrianople, where he'd just written to all the kings and rulers, including those of America. By now, Bahá'u'lláh had very powerful enemies who were angered that his prestige was growing yet again. Even conniving members of his own family, his half-brother and other relatives, were involved in treachery, blinded by their jealousy of the esteem and adoration showered on him by his followers and a growing number of important people. Sultan 'Abdu'l-'Azíz, goaded into action, further banished Bahá'u'lláh to the penal colony of 'Akká, right here on the shores of the Mediterranean.

"Bahá'u'lláh and about 70 companions arrived by sailboat at the sea gate of 'Akká, in the pulsing summer heat of August 31st, 1868. Bahá'u'lláh's wife Navváb and their young, 'Abbás, Bahíyyih, and Mihdi, were with him. It was scorching, and they all suffered.

"So, Bahá'u'lláh and his bedraggled companions, now known as Bahá'ís, were all herded through the narrow, stinking streets to the Prison. They were pelted with stones and filth by the irate citizens who lined the streets, who'd been told they were heretics. 'Akká was a terrible place, so foul and filthy that birds dropped dead out of the sky from the stench."

"Why was it so foul, Lumina?" asks Sophie, turning a bit green.

" 'Akká is a seaport, Sophie, and for centuries ships from all over the Mediterranean have docked here and off-loaded. The caravans awaiting their new trade stayed in caravanserais, which were big, open quadrangles, like open-air motels. As all those camels and mules moved around, they left heaps of ... 'souvenirs' all over the place. The streets were never cleaned, unless it rained, and then it all ran in the gutters. Get the picture?"

"Eeeuuuuu!" Sophie, turns greener with repugnance.

Lumina draws Eric and Sophie close to him, and zooms them in on the courtyard of the Prison. Ping! They watch as Bahá'u'lláh, his family and followers, trudge up the long staircase into the dank, dark interior. Inside, the clamour is deafening, as the guards yell at the hapless Bahá'ís. Dirty water and moldy bread is all they're given to eat after their terrible journey.

But then a quiet descends as Bahá'u'lláh's strong voice rings out in prayer, and the overwhelming misery of his loved ones is soothed, eased, transformed for the moment into serenity. Sophie lifts her light-face, rapt, drinking in the sound of his reverberating chanting. She has never before heard anything like it. She feels such vibrations of power surging through her light-body, charging her being with a tremendous feeling of strength.

"Bahá'u'lláh called this 'the Most Great Prison', Light Knights," says Lumina, as they emerge, a bit dazed, from the darkness into the light. "They suffered untold misery here; some of them died."

"I'm amazed at the cruelty and utter, crass blindness of the Sultan, Lumina."

"The Sultan and the Shah had only one agenda, Eric: to get rid of Bahá'u'lláh and his perpetual challenge. The strange thing is, they kept removing Bahá'u'lláh instead of killing him outright. In so doing, they unwittingly fulfilled all sorts of prophesies. They brought Bahá'u'lláh to the very spot that the Bible foretold. His journey had brought him from the east, over the mountains, from sea to sea, and finally to the plains of Sharon of the Holy Land[12]. Eventually he would pitch his tent on GOD's holy mountain, Mount Carmel."

"Boy! They should've been more afraid of GOD. They really never gave GOD a thought, did they? GOD did get them, though, didn't He!"

"They got their just rewards, Sophie. So, although he was imprisoned, Bahá'u'lláh stayed in contact with his followers. He wrote from his prison cell to the believers in Persia. And he waved a handkerchief from his cell window to the hopeful pilgrims who came on foot to catch a glimpse of him. However, his enemies were everywhere, so they were never allowed to see or visit him."

"Lumina, you did mention that his own brother was in on the scheming against Bahá'u'lláh. It's terrible the way jealousy just curdles and eats away at your soul. It reminds me of Joseph's brothers all over again."

"That's right, Eric. Down through the ages the story of the Covenant has always been shot through with adversity and betrayal. The world is a hard, resistant place, and the new teachings take hold only through trials and hardship. After all, there has to be corruption for a solution to be necessary, right?"

"Did Bahá'u'lláh ever get out of prison?"

"He did, Sophie. But, I have to tell you that a terrible accident happened before that. Mihdi, who was about twenty now, was walking on the roof, sunk in deep thought and meditation, when he crashed through a skylight and fell on shards on the floor beneath. As Bahá'u'lláh held his dying son in his arms, Mihdi begged him to let him go, to let his death open the doors of the Prison. It was an agonizing moment for father and son."

Sophie raises her mournful light-eyes to Lumina's, absorbing the pain, thinking about sad parents everywhere, her own, too .... She sighs and turns to Eric. He nods quietly; he understands, too.

Lumina goes on. "It seems incredible, Sophie, but the prison doors did open. The Turks needed the barracks to billet their army, so Bahá'u'lláh's family was moved about until they finally came to rest at the home of 'Abbúd, and that's where Bahá'u'lláh wrote his Book of Laws designed to bring peace and justice to the world."

"But how could Bahá'u'lláh *do* anything?" asks Sophie. "He was still a prisoner, wasn't he? The Sultan sure didn't say he was free."

# 29 THE COVENANT FLIES FREE

"There were so many people coming and going, Sophie. The Bahá'ís were teaching Bahá'u'lláh's new faith all over Persia, Turkey and Iraq. And it spread to Russia, India, Egypt, and beyond. Scholars in Europe were curious, and one Englishman, Dr. Granville Browne, even visited Bahá'u'lláh at Bahjí, his final home out in the countryside, after nine years imprisoned within the walls of the squalid city of 'Akká. "

"What did Bahá'u'lláh say to the doctor?"

"Sophie, Dr. Browne was a scholar in Eastern studies, and he could speak Persian. He quoted Bahá'u'lláh as saying:

'Praise be to God that thou has attained! ... Thou hast come to see a prisoner and an exile ... We desire but the good of the world and happiness of the nations; yet they deem us a stirrer up of strife and sedition worthy of bondage and banishment ... Yet so it shall be; these fruitless strifes, these ruinous wars shall pass away, and the 'Most Great Peace' shall come ....' [13]

"So," Lumina continued, "Bahá'u'lláh was really talking about the Kingdom of GOD when he spoke of this Most Great Peace, wasn't he?"

"And, the doctor, Lumina, he must've felt *something,*" Sophie says earnestly. "I mean, he was talking to the Promised One!"

"He did describe his own feeling of wonderment. He wrote, 'No need to ask in whose presence I stood, as I bowed myself before one who is the object of a devotion and love which kings might envy and emperors sigh for in vain!'[14]

Sophie, nods quietly as Lumina continues. "So, now, getting back to our story, no matter what the Sultan or the Shah did, nothing stopped the hope, joy, and fervor of the Bahá'ís from spreading like wildfire.

"The day came, in 1892, when Bahá'u'lláh died quietly at Bahjí, his work in the Earth World complete. Now the mantle passed to his son, 'Abbás, who became known as 'Abdu'l-Bahá, 'the Servant of Bahá', after Bahá'u'lláh died. It was up to him to continue his father's work and to foster unity among the believers. He was called the Centre of the Covenant."

"Woohoo! The Covenant rides again!"

"That it did, Sophie! So, time went by, with lots more huge problems to be overcome, but finally, in 1908, the Sultan of Turkey was deposed by the revolution of the 'Young Turks'."

"*Yeess!* The people speak! Be gone, you black-hearted, cruel Sultan, and all your nasty henchmen!"

The brothers smile at Sophie.

Lumina continues. "The Young Turks took power and freed the religious and political prisoners right across the Ottoman Empire. And that, of course, included 'Abdu'l- Bahá. Now something very wonderful happened. Bahá'u'lláh, before he died, had shown 'Abdu'l- Bahá exactly where, on Mount Carmel, the body of the Báb was to be buried. Remember how the Báb was executed back in 1850? Well, his remains had been secretly hidden away all those years.

"'Abdu'l-Bahá now lived in Haifa, across the bay from the prison city of 'Akká, and he had a tomb built on the exact spot Bahá'u'lláh had shown him, on the slopes of Mount Carmel, facing the Mediterranean Sea. On the Bahá'í New Year, *Naw-Rúz*, the 21st of March, in 1909, he fulfilled this most precious trust, and interred the remains of the Báb in the heart of Carmel, the ancient Mountain of GOD."

All three Light Knights reflect, for a moment, on the peace and wonder of this extraordinary event.

"Lumina," says Eric, quietly, "all the suffering, so much sorrow, and danger, everything always hanging by a thread .... 'Abdu'l-Bahá must've lived it all in that moment."

"He did, Eric. 'Abdu'l-Bahá wept with such a great weeping that those who were present wept with him. If our Quest has shown us anything, it's that the path of the Covenant has always been a journey from crisis to ultimate victory."

"GOD finally did it!" Sophie is pummeling the air, light-arms swinging.

"Well, it's not over yet, Sophie! 'Abdu'l-Bahá worked incessantly, reaching out to everyone, writing copiously to all the Bahá'ís around the world, explaining his father's teachings, encouraging them, and showering them with love. Since Bahá'u'lláh's day, the Bahá'í Faith had spread through Europe to America. New believers from America came to visit 'Abdu'l-Bahá, begging him to come to their country. So, in 1912, now an old man, 'Abdu'l-Bahá travelled all the way from Palestine to Egypt, France, England and Scotland, and then on to the United States and Canada.

"Can you believe it? He carried Bahá'u'lláh's Message across the western world! And everywhere he went, people flocked to him."

"Wow!" says Sophie. "It's like GOD walked across the ocean to *us*!"

# 30 THE KINGDOM UNFOLDS

"Yes, Sophie, and what a remarkable visit it was, over many months, from coast to coast across America, bringing the Message of Bahá'u'lláh—one of unity, hope, divine justice and world peace. 'Abdu'l-Bahá touched countless hearts, meeting high and low alike, his all-encompassing love flowing out to every corner of America.

"And then, nine years later in Haifa, 'Abdu'l-Bahá laid down his weary head and departed from the Earth World. However, he left a written *Will and Testament*. This document and Bahá'u'lláh's Holy Book, the *Kitab'i'Aqdas*, his Book of Laws, contain the 'blueprint' for building a whole new world."

"You mean there's a *real* plan, Lumina? On paper?" Sophie is amazed.

"There sure is, Sophie, and it's huge. The Plan I'm talking about is designed to transform the globe, uniting all humanity in one common faith. Do you see, Sophie?"

"You bet I see!"

"But good intentions alone won't be enough to unite humanity; it'll take effort and organization, and that's what the Plan is all about. 'Abdu'l-Bahá named his oldest grandson, young Shoghi Effendi, as the Guardian of the

Bahá'í Faith, and he became the master-builder. He took Bahá'u'lláh's blueprint, and over the next 26 years he communicated tirelessly with all the Bahá'ís world-wide, mapping out the Plan. Millions of people adopted this new faith. He chose helpers, 'Hands of the Cause', to guide these new communities that were blooming on every continent, and he sent the Bahá'ís out on crusades!"

"*Crusades*?" cries Sophie. Her light-curls are standing right up on end.

"Well, these ones were teaching crusades, Sophie. Remember that Bahá'u'lláh put the power in the hands of the people. There's no clergy in his faith, so the blueprint called for the Bahá'ís to elect local and national governing bodies to shepherd their affairs. The glue for their unity is obedience to Bahá'u'lláh's laws and teachings. As the framework grew and strengthened, the Bahá'ís knew they were preparing for the eventual election of the Universal House of Justice to govern their affairs internationally. Then the Bahá'í blueprint would be complete, and Bahá'u'lláh's spiritual principles would flow irreversibly into the whole world.

"For decades Shoghi Effendi toiled over his maps and charts, writing, guiding, encouraging the Bahá'ís world-wide. He translated many of the texts of Bahá'u'lláh and 'Abdu'l-Bahá into English, a language he commanded perfectly, having studied at Oxford University in England before 'Abdu'l-Bahá died.

"So, do you see how the whole world is being tied together, Sophie?"

"I see GOD, GOD, *GOD* all over the place. Lumina, this Quest has made GOD soooo real for me." Sophie's light-body glows brighter, expanding again.

"I don't want this to end, Lumina." Eric sighs.

"It's not over yet! Shoghi Effendi died suddenly in 1957 when he was in England. Search as they might, the Hands couldn't find a will naming a new Guardian, so it was time for the Universal House of Justice to be born."

"Amazing how it's all happening so fast!" remarks Eric.

"After a tremendous world-wide effort by all the Bahá'ís, they completed the goals of Shoghi Effendi's last teaching crusade, and on April 21, 1963, all the elected national bodies existing in the Bahá'í world gathered in Haifa to elect the first Universal House of Justice. This was just one hundred years after Bahá'u'lláh declared his mission to his followers in the Garden of Ridván. The blueprint was complete.

"Then Bahá'ís from around the world flocked to London, England, where Shoghi Effendi died and is buried. Thousands of Bahá'ís gathered for a great World Congress to celebrate this earth-changing moment. The peoples of the world assembled in joy and gratitude from every continent; from the islands of the Pacific; from the north, south, east and west. It was a spectacle of traditional costumes from all over the globe. These were the people who had helped complete the Guardian's work. An incredibly powerful moment in the Bahá'í world – in the whole world!"

"So Planet Earth has become a bubbling laboratory!" Eric sums it up. "You're right, Sophie! GOD did it!"

"Woohoo!" she shouts, gleefully.

Eric grins at her from light-ear to light-ear. "Sophie, I love ya!"

"You knew all this, Eric?"

"Oh, Lord, no! I only knew parts of the story. So, Lumina, where do we go from here? Our Quest has been accomplished, right? We found the

Promised One foretold again and again over thousands of years. The Covenant of GOD has been fulfilled, hasn't it?"

"It's just another beginning, Light Knights. Because of the new spirit of unity let loose, the Earth World is going through the most painful and powerful transformation it's ever experienced. Even the weather is worked up, with storms, earthquakes and volcanic eruptions happening more and more frequently. The whole balance of the Earth is changing. The Maya calendar is ushering in a brand new Cycle. And the Time of the End foretold in the Bible, and by Zoroaster, Krishna, the Buddha, and Muhammad, has arrived. Now, as Bahá'u'lláh's teachings take effect through the work of countless souls, we'll see how the powers of evil will be chained up.

"No matter what happens to the planet, one thing's for sure—it's transforming, not disappearing. The 'Cycle of Prophecy' has been completed, and Bahá'u'lláh has initiated a new 'Cycle of Unity' that will endure 500,000 years. Imagine! That can only mean one thing: the search may be over, but the work of the Covenant, building the Most Great Peace, the Kingdom of GOD on earth, has now begun in earnest, and will go on for eons to come."

With that, Lumina swooshes them to the slopes of Mount Carmel. "Light Knights, when Bahá'u'lláh walked on Mount Carmel, it was nothing but stones and wilderness. But now look at it! It's a garden, the centre of the work of the Kingdom. See the beautiful Shrine of the Báb over there? Its glowing, golden dome and gorgeous terraces stretch from the street below right up to the summit of Mount Carmel. Kings and leaders will one day climb those steps to ask the Universal House of Justice for guidance. Just try to picture it!"

Lumina then extends his light-arms towards some beautiful classical buildings situated along a sweeping arc. "Those are the buildings of the Bahá'í World Centre, designed by the very same Bahá'í architect who designed the 'Tower of Remembrance of the Kings' in Tehran."

"Oh my gosh," exclaims Sophie. "So the person who designed that amazing tower was a Bahá'í? The same people who were so persecuted! That's perfect."

Eric is thinking about the future, all the spiritual energy and guidance that has flowed, and continues to flow, from the Holy Land, this wonderful hub of Planet Earth. "I can feel this Message of unity travelling out on the air waves," remarks Eric, "invading every part of the Earth World—like a *healthy* virus! Once GOD released the power through Bahá'u'lláh, nothing could stop it, eh?

"So really, humanity is coming to grips with the biggest misconception in history. We're *not* born imperfect and incapable of conquering our lower instincts. No way! We're all created in the image of GOD, noble to the core, and capable of reaching up and doing enormous good. We can do it!

"Lumina, I see war as a terrible betrayal of that inner spirit. Is it any wonder soldiers return from the battlefields with their souls crushed, everything sacred brutalized? We're spiritual beings! And when we finally see that, and turn to GOD and His Messenger, everything will change, won't it? They say it takes a shift of just one percent of the population to change the direction of the whole world? I'm sure up for *that*, Lumina!"

"Good on ya, Eric! Sophie, now do you understand that our job, as Light Knights, is to help this process in the Earth World? That's why we exist, and why you've joined Eric and me on this Quest?"

Sophie nods, beaming radiantly, her bright, golden light sending out shafts in all directions.

"Bahá'u'lláh brought principles and solutions for all the woes and troubles worrying us and every youth out there. He brought laws to equip us, just like armour, giving us moral strength. Youth can dare to be different, truthful, and strong, with help from us Light Knights. We can give the youth the courage to face challenges, and to be pure and noble. These days, the youth need lots of encouragement to keep free of drugs, bad habits, and temptations that mess up our minds and bodies."

Eric jumps in. "Yeah, Lumina, that's for sure. But some are already in big trouble, addicted to drugs or involved in crime, or maybe running away from bad situations at home. Even getting involved in extremist groups because they see no hope. We need to help them too—*especially* them!"

Eric pauses, thoughtful. "And it's really important for us youth to figure out that love is a virtue that belongs to the soul, the light-body, because when the hormones kick in, love takes on a whole new meaning, eh? It's important to realize that hormones belong to the earth-body so we don't get love and hormones muddled. Our minds, our light-bodies, need to be running the show, keeping things under control, so that our hormones don't take over."

"Well put, Eric. All youth have lots of capacity to take charge of themselves and be strong, armed with the courage and determination to make a difference. So, Light Knights, we have to work hard to support and inspire all the Earth Knights!"

"You know," says Sophie, "my mom and dad didn't talk about GOD, but they sure talked a lot about helping the world. They wanted me to think hard about what I wanted to be when I grew up; they hoped I'd choose something that would make a difference, a good difference. One thing that made Mom cry was that I'd never grow up. She thought I was being robbed of my life by dying so young.

"Lumina, do I really have the power to help the Earth World change from here?" She's gazing at them both with her big brown light-eyes. "Remember? I tried to reach my earth family, but I couldn't seem to get through to them. How am I going to help anyone else if I can't help them?"

"Sophie, something has happened since then!"

"What do you mean? To *me*?"

# 31 FAITH IS LIFE

"Don't you see it, Sophie? You've been talking about it all along. See how your light-body has changed from rosy to gold? That's your soul all lit up! And do you know why?" Eric is eyeing her expectantly.

"Oh, Eric, I do-I do-I *do!*" Sophie dances joyfully. "It's the GOD thing, isn't it? Because I'm connected to GOD! No wonder I've turned gold! And my soul, my divine light-body—it's awake and loving GOD back. I feel that." Her joy sends out a spray of golden sparks.

"Ah, that's the secret! When we're connected to GOD, we have *real* power. Now you'll make a difference!" Lumina grins proudly at Sophie.

"Woohoo! I'm light, light, light ...." Sophie whirls around creating a little cyclone of sparks. "So? Now what happens? Do thoughts reach us from the Earth World?"

"That's what prayers are all about, Sophie," explains Eric. "Sometimes they're quiet; sometimes they're screams for help. We can reach people in their quiet moments and just zap a thought to them. At other times, we meet them in their dreams and help them find solutions. Then there are moments when we seem to come out of thin air, just there when it's least expected and most needed.

"It's a two way street, see? It's all positive love, light, and understanding, this GOD power that operates between the worlds. But people have to turn to GOD on purpose to get plugged in. The Messengers have relayed that Message forever; but we have to obey the Message. Imagine how powerful the GOD power would be in the Earth World if everyone tuned in to Bahá'u'lláh's solutions? That's how we can help, Sophie."

"I'm game! Count me in! I don't want to lose you guys, no way!" Sophie wraps her light-arms around her buddies, spinning them into a glowing huddle.

"Be prepared, Light Knights! See all those flashes going off?" Out goes Lumina's light-arm. "Those are signals from the Earth World—prayers! They know we're here, at their service, ready to zoom in at any moment. There's no separation between the Light World and the Earth World, and, man—they're tuning in."

"Look!" Lumina extends his light arm in the opposite direction. "See those light-bodies zooming off? Countless Light Knights like us are helping all the time!"

"Lumina, I'm so proud to be a Light Knight. Thank you, thank you, *thank* you! Eric, just look at me—I've grown up! I'm so wickedly bright—hahaaa!" Sophie flings her light-arms out, spinning golden joy.

So, beware, all you unsuspecting earthlings! There's a Light Knight named Sophie on the loose! She's not the same light-body that first arrived in the Light World, no siree.

"We'll do it, Sophie!" Eric beams. "'Mission *Possible*', eh? Thanks a million, Lumina, my buddy, my bro—you're the best! I love ya both!"

"Ready for the next assignment, Light Knights?" Lumina asks. "To help all those Earth Knights out there? There are millions like us all set to go, just waiting to plug in and change the Earth World, and we'll be right in there. Assignment Earth World coming up! Contact ... let's go! *Quest-Hoooo!*"

PPHHhhhSSssssstttTT

And there go our wonderful Sophie and her buddies, Lumina and Eric, spreading the light, answering the flashes. Is one of them from you?

# THOUGHTS AND THANKS

Now my pen is stilled, the results of my mental mulling, research and long hours of hard work finally on paper. I am grateful to so many people for their help in bringing this book to light. Thank you to Adrian, my husband, for reading and commenting at so many stages of its development, to Cherie Winslow and other dear friends who encouraged me with their suggestions along the way, often unleashing a whole chain of new ideas. I wish to particularly thank Suzanne Maloney and her husband Julian Lebensold whose in-depth critiques of the first draft of the book led to the maturing of the text from its very tentative and embryonic state. Without their knowledge and probing questions the book could never have developed as it did. And, thank you to Liam, our 14-year-old grandson, who later read the matured text, and offered his very necessary and perceptive comments as a youth, the very audience I have targeted. I also thank our daughter, Robin, a wee bit older, who did the same. I was delighted with all their feed-back. To Judy Tompkins, my editor, who launched herself heart and soul into the demanding work of tidying up my prose and punctuation, with pertinent comments and amendments, my undying gratitude and praise. As well, with a huge sigh of relief, my thanks to the National Spiritual Assembly of the Bahá'ís of Canada, whose Literature Committee diligently reviewed the text and gave it their 'seal of approval'. And, also, to friends Phyllis and Bill Webster, who have kindly done the final proof-reading with patience and a meticulous eye, thank you!

With regards to the design of the book, my gratitude to Louise Després Jones for her initial work. She evoked Sophie's Light World vividly. In an effort to redesign, to appeal to a broader audience, we ran out of time, and Del Carry stepped up to the plate. Thank you Del. It is my hope that this simpler approach appeals to all readers, boys and girls, youth and older, and that the narrative comes to life in their minds as vividly as it did for Louise.

I have included a very short list for Further Reading, along with a few

End Notes, which might prove useful. Of course, the internet is boundless. The ultimate goal of this book is to provoke curiosity and personal research, that primary principle of 'investigation of the truth'. I hope it succeeds.

And now I am going to share something very special with you. It was the vivid dream of my very dear friend, Navid Naimi, as I mentioned in 'Setting the Scene', that convinced me to write the book and set the text in the Light World. Navid died of cancer this past spring, on the anniversary of our Eric's accident and death, April 30th, and I was destined to be at her bedside when she flew away. These are mysteries we do not understand, so humbling, and so very significant. I cherish Navid's friendship profoundly, and am grateful for the encouragement she gave me as I shared the ideas of the book along the way. I have felt her radiant spirit as I worked. So, now she is with Eric and Lumina who, I am convinced, were 'assigned' to their mum for this project. How many times I suddenly thought of important things to say, how often I laughed aloud as I 'heard' their voices prodding me to action. I have tried to put it all into words, however inadequate. Thank you to my two light-boys. And finally, my eternal gratitude to Bahá'u'lláh whose teachings have stirred my innermost being to the core. I hope I have conveyed something of the grandeur and wonder of his teachings to you.

I wrote this book for our grandchildren and their children to come. I wrote this book for all youthful souls who are searching. I wrote this book for you.

'Mugiemoss', Hudson, Québec, Canada, February 2014.

# END NOTES

1. Gleanings from the Writings of Bahá'u'lláh, p. 217 . . . . . . . . 9
2. Genesis 22:18 . . . . . . . . . . . . . . . . . . . . 52
3. Isaiah 53:7 . . . . . . . . . . . . . . . . . . . . 90
4. Isaiah 9:6-7 . . . . . . . . . . . . . . . . . . . . 90
5. Qur'an 42:13 . . . . . . . . . . . . . . . . . . . . 101
6. Summons of the Lord of Hosts, p. 6 . . . . . . . . . . . . 125
7. The Promised Day is Come, p. 66 . . . . . . . . . . . . 132
8. Gleanings from the Writings of Bahá'u'lláh, p. 136 . . . . . . . 134
9. The Kitáb-i-Aqdas, p. 2 . . . . . . . . . . . . . . . 135
10. Gleanings from the Writings of Bahá'u'lláh, p. 313 . . . . . . . 135
11. Ibid, p. 136 . . . . . . . . . . . . . . . . . . . . 140
12. Isaiah 35:2 . . . . . . . . . . . . . . . . . . . . 145
13. Bahá'u'lláh and the New Era, p. 39-40 . . . . . . . . . . . 147
14. Ibid, p. 39 . . . . . . . . . . . . . . . . . . . . 148

# FURTHER READING


Boyce, Mary, *Zoroastrianism: Its Antiquity and Constant Vigour;* California, Mazda Publishers, 1992.

De Bary, Wm. Theodore, *Sources of Indian Tradition, vol. 1;* New York, Columbia Press, 1958.

Effendi, Shoghi, *God Passes By;* Wilmette, Ill., Bahá'í Publishing Trust, 1965.

Esselmont, J.E., *Bahá'u'lláh and the New Era: An Introduction to the Bahá'í Faith;* Wilmette, Ill., Bahá'í Publishing Trust, 1970.

Gibb, H.A.R., *Mohammedanism: An Historical Survey;* New York, Oxford Press, 1970.

Gilbert, Adrian G. and Cotterell, Maurice M., *The Mayan Prophecies: Unlocking the Secrets of a Lost Civilization;* Rockport, MA, Element Books Ltd., 1996.

Hopkins, Peter, *Foreign Devils on the Silk Road;* Oxford, Oxford University Press, 1980.

Niderost, Heather I., *The Myth of Maitreya in Modern Japan: with a History of its Evolution;* Montréal, Faculty of Religious Studies, McGill University, 1992.

Rahula, Walpola, *What the Buddha Taught;* New York, Grove Press Inc., 1974.

*The New Annotated Bible;* Oxford, Oxford University Press, 1977.

Willoya, William and Brown, Vinson; *Warriors of the Rainbow: Strange Prophetic Dreams of the Indian Peoples;* California, Naturegraph Publishers Inc., 1962.

# ABOUT THE AUTHOR

Heather Niderost (née Attridge) was born in Montréal, Canada. In 1961 she received her B.A. from McGill University and married Adrian Carl Niderost, a mechanical engineer and recipient of an Athlone Fellowship, which took them to Britain. There the author earned her teaching certificate from the Aberdeen College of Education and her Diploma of Education from St. Mary's College, University of Aberdeen, Scotland. Aberdeen was also where she and her husband encountered the Bahá'í Faith. In 1963, they returned to Canada and raised a family of five. Their fourth child, Eric, who was killed in an accident in 1981, was the focus of Heather's first book, *The Light World*. She is also the author of *A Pilgrim's Song,* written in 1998. In 1992, Heather earned an M.A. at McGill University in Comparative Religious Studies, which led to this present book. After many years of living and travelling abroad, they now divide their time between Montréal and Métis-sur-Mer, Québec.

# OTHER BOOKS BY AUTHOR

*Available at:* bookstore.bahai.ca (all categories, Heather I Niderost)

## THE LIGHT WORLD

This little book was first published nearly 20 years ago, and it is as timely today as it was then. It talks about life after death. It recounts the author's experience of losing her ten year old son, Eric, but it is Eric's voice we hear. He tells his readers, young or old, how he died and, through the aegis of the Bahá'í Writings, what life and death are all about. Its objective is "to remove the fear of death from the minds of our children." It is a truly happy book! It has helped many, many families, and continues its healing journey.

## A PILGRIM'S SONG

Pilgrimage to the Bahá'í World Centre, the burial place of its 3 central figures and its world administrative centre, is for Bahá'ís, and many others, a profoundly moving experience. Come share this wonderful voyage as it unfolds through the narrative and illustrations—feel the atmosphere, the moments that inspired writing "The Light World."

57424905R00095

Made in the USA
Charleston, SC
13 June 2016